GLASGOW

GLASGOW

PORTRAITS OF A CITY

ALLAN MASSIE

BARRIE & JENKINS

LONDON

First published in Great Britain in 1989 by
Barrie & Jenkins Ltd
289 Westbourne Grove, London W11 2QA

British Library Cataloguing in Publication Data

Massie, Allan, *1938–*
    Glasgow.
    1. Scotland. Strathclyde region. Glasgow, history
    I. Title
    941.4'43

    ISBN 0-7126-2054-0

Typeset by DP Photosetting, Aylesbury, Bucks
Printed in Great Britain by
Richard Clay Ltd, Bungay, Suffolk

FOR MY MOTHER AND FATHER.

CONTENTS

LIST OF ILLUSTRATIONS

PHOTOGRAPHIC CREDITS

T & R Annan: 2, 3a, 3b, 4, 5, 9, 11a; Allsport: 14a; Douglas Corrance: 14b; Malcolm Fife, Edinburgh Photographic Library: 16; Fotomas Index: 1a, 1b; *Glasgow Herald* and *Evening Times*: 8a, 8b, 11; Glasgow Museums and Art Galleries: 12b; Hulton-Deutsch Collection: 6, 10, 12a; Mitchell Library (Glasgow Room): endpapers; David Morrison, Edinburgh Photographic Library: 15; People's Palace, Glasgow Museums and Art Galleries: 13; Strathclyde Regional Archives: 7.

CHAPTER ONE

COLOURS RESTORED

In 1977 a young writer, Alan Spence, published a collection of short stories called *Its Colours They Are Fine*. The title comes from the marching song 'The Sash', which is the principal anthem of the Orange Order. Spence was born into a Protestant working-class family in Govan, that old village across the Clyde from the centre of Glasgow, the home of shipyards and Rangers football club. These stories, which deal with the childhood, adolescence and early manhood of a group of boys, offer a notable imaginative re-creation of working-class life in the city in the 1950s and 1960s. They are Spence's response to a Glasgow of deprivation and violence, squalor, dislocation and hopelessness. It is a city in which communities that had a life of their own have been destroyed in the benevolent name of social progress, in which tens of thousands of people have been decanted to bleak housing estates that peel, crumble and stain almost before they are finished, where the centre reminds one of photographs of post-war Berlin, where religion is expressed only in sectarian animosity, and where reality is to be found in football, the boozer and the dance-hall. Perhaps most bitter of all is the way in which Spence shows how the natural and affectionate enthusiasms of childhood fade, to be replaced either by a narrow and brutal coarseness or by escapist experiments through drugs, oriental religion or, that old stand-by, alcohol.

When I reviewed this book in 1977 I wrote admiringly of it and observed that it was a commonplace that periods of material decline were often culturally rich and no city in Britain, or perhaps Europe, was so evidently decaying as Glasgow.

The judgement seemed fair. Glasgow had long lost its position as 'the second city of the Empire', had indeed done so even before the Empire itself disappeared. Its great industry, shipbuilding, was in decay. The city that had build a third of the world's merchant fleet before 1914 now struggled to win orders for ships, and then was hard put to fulfil any that were won. Its population was falling, partly as a result of policy, partly as a consequence of economic decline. Its unemployment rate was much above the national average.

In certain respects, it is true, life in the city was materially better for most of its citizens. Literary evidence is never exact, but can still be used as a guide. A comparison of Spence's stories with the novel *No Mean City* (1935) by Alexander McArthur and H. Kingsley Long – later filmed – would establish that poverty and squalor are always relative. If Spence's Glasgow seemed mean when set against contemporary conditions in other British cities, it was very much better than the place portrayed in the earlier fiction, where razor gangs fought pitched battles in Gorbals streets, and the tenement dwellers could be described by the not entirely unsympathetic authors as if they belonged to another order of humanity. Physical conditions had improved likewise. Spence's housing schemes and multi-storey blocks might be bleak enough; they were better than the tenements of the old Gorbals, of which McArthur and Long could write:

> Cavity beds are so common a feature of the Glasgow slums even to this day that the tenement dwellers take them for granted. The ordinary 'room-and-kitchen' apartment, and even the one-roomed 'single-end', always includes a cavity bed or beds. These beds are no more than windowless closets – little tombs about five feet by five by three and a half. The door of each closes against the side of the bed and flush with the wall of the room itself.

It was no wonder that death-rates, especially infant mortality, were so high. John Wheatley, the first Labour Minister of Health, published a table of infant deaths in different parts of the city, and observed that 'you may see at a glance that the infant death-rate in working-class wards is three, four and almost five times higher than in Kelvinside'. Overcrowding in Glasgow right up to the Second World War was between five and ten times greater than in corresponding English cities. Even by 1951, however, there were still two people living in one room in 15.5 per cent of houses in Scotland compared with 2.1 per cent in England and Wales. The figure in Glasgow was higher still.

These appalling figures which made Glasgow slums the worst north of Naples – and far less tolerable than those of Naples – were the city's shame. They were also the consequence of its success, and of the nature of that success. Glasgow had grown so rapidly, so early, and had been so flooded by Highland and Irish immigrants eager to share in its economic expansion that social provision lagged far behind industrial development. Moreover, inasmuch as Glasgow's nineteenth-century economic miracle was based partly on a low-wage economy, the opportunity for the workers to improve their living conditions by their own efforts was, in consequence, limited.

Ever since the Industrial Revolution poverty, squalor, ill-health and early death have been the lot of the greater part of the population of Glasgow. Yet, throughout the nineteenth century, two considerations might restrain indignant judgement. First, however wretched the existence of the Glasgow poor, it was not necessarily more miserable than the one they had known in the rural world from which they had fled to Glasgow, nor indeed was it more precarious; if they encountered squalor in the city, they had known famine in the countryside. For the Irish immigrants who swarmed into the city in the 1840s, Glasgow offered a refuge and held out hope. They were dying in Ireland as a result of the potato blight; they might live in Glasgow. Indeed, as the historian Sydney Checkland put it:

> It should be remembered that many who came to the crowded tenements of Glasgow from Irish cabins, Hebridean black houses or continental ghettoes found them to be an improvement. It might also be remembered that conditions in the new industrial cities of England, Europe and the United States were little, if any, better than in Glasgow.

Second, Glasgow was a city of opportunity, being carried forward on a seemingly unbreakable wave of expansion and optimism. If many of its poorest remained miserably poor, others advanced to relative prosperity. A skilled workman in Glasgow in 1900 lived very much better than his equivalent a hundred years earlier. He was aware, too, of the opportunities for further improvement, and all round him he saw evidence of the greatness of his city. He had a sense of momentum.

By the time Alan Spence came to write his book, this sense had been lost. Yet, as the city's economic vigour abated and Glasgow sank from being a cause for wonder to a cause for concern, the material circumstances of its citizens steadily improved. By 1970 an unemployed man experienced a standard of living far higher than even a skilled workman might have enjoyed a hundred years earlier. Yet this development had less to do with conditions in Glasgow itself than with the diffusion of wealth and the creation of systems of social welfare common to the whole Western world.

Yet, whatever material benefits the twentieth century brought Glasgow – and they were real – they could not compensate in the eyes of its citizens for what had been lost. One of the most distressing features of periods of unemployment is offered by the middle-aged man who realises that he will be unlikely to work again; in the 1970s Glasgow resembled that man; there was reason to fear that the city would not function again.

A change has come over Glasgow within the last twelve years or so.

Materially, many in the city may be no better-off – some indeed are worse-off as a result of the high levels of unemployment which have persisted in certain areas for most of the last decade. Yet that fear that Glasgow had lost its function, and might not find a new one, has disappeared. The city is buoyant again, confident of its future. Periods in history are never clear-cut; the seeds of revival were sown in the worst years. But the change of mood and of the manner in which Glasgow addresses the world is distinctive. My judgement of 1977 – that no city in Britain, or perhaps Europe, was so evidently decaying as Glasgow – looks as absurd in retrospect as it seemed realistic when I wrote it. If anyone had suggested then, that Glasgow might be nominated as Cultural Capital of Europe, he or she would have been ridiculed. When the nomination was made ten years later, for 1990, it was hailed not only as splendid, but more remarkably, as reasonable.

This is not a history of Glasgow, though I have set it in a historical form. It offers a series of portraits of the city at different times. It might, at best, be termed a 'historical sketch' or 'notes towards an appreciation of the city'. I have tried to show what Glasgow has meant to different people at different times, for a great city is always an idea – or dream of possibilities – as well as an object. I have tried to show how the interplay of culture and economic functions forms that idea and stimulates that dream and, at the same time, to give some sense of what it felt like to live in Glasgow at different times.

CHAPTER TWO

FOUNDATION TO UNION

Glasgow can boast of a history stretching back into the dark ages. For more than a thousand years, however, reasons of geography and the logic of historical development made it of secondary importance. Then it became a creative force, a motor that drove unprecedented economic expansion. Throughout most of the city's history, Scotland looked east to the continent of Europe: the Baltic, the north German ports of the Hanseatic League, the Netherlands and France were the points of entry and contact. They were served by Leith, Aberdeen, Dundee and the little ports of the East Neuk of Fife. Glasgow could have no part in this. Nor was it of military importance. No great battles were fought in its immediate vicinity. Only one decisive skirmish – the Battle of Langside (1568), which saw the extinction of Mary Stewart's last hope of maintaining herself in Scotland – was fought there. It was only when Scotland turned to the Atlantic and the open seas in the eighteenth century that Glasgow came into her own.

Geography accounts for the city's comparative insignificance. The hills come down to the northern fringes of the modern city. The firth leads to the open sea, but this was unfrequented, except during the centuries of the Viking raiders, until the eighteenth century. The Clyde, curling down from the Lanarkshire hills, was neither a navigable waterway nor a strategic barrier, for the routes which an army might ordinarily take passed to the east of it. To the south, admittedly, Glasgow opens to the rich farmlands of Ayrshire, but this county was itself isolated by geography.

One institution, however, helped Glasgow flourish in the centuries before the Reformation. This was the Church. Medieval Glasgow, of which so little survives, derived its importance from its standing as an episcopal see. The city owes its origins to the impulses of religion.

The sixth-century founder, and the city's patron saint was Mungo, otherwise known as Kentigern. According to his biographer, a twelfth-century monk Jocelyn from the Cistercian monastery of Furness, which was then within the diocese of Glasgow, he was the son of a king of Cumbria and of Thenaw, daughter of King Loth of Traprain in Lothian. This Loth is the King Lot of the Arthurian legends, whom the medieval historical romancer Geoffrey of Monmouth, writing half a century before Jocelyn, called variously the brother-in-law and uncle by marriage of Arthur; he was the father of Gawaine and Mordred. This is not the only point which connects St Mungo with the Arthurian story.

Unfortunately the King of Cumbria had seduced Thenaw but failed to marry her. She was therefore set adrift from the Bass Rock in a little boat, which, in a reversal of fortune, came ashore at Culross in Fife, where St Serf, a disciple of St Palladius, had established a monastery. The illegitimate child was born and raised there, and educated in the Faith. His mother was later to be canonised, her shame being obliterated by the glory of her son. In the Middle Ages a chapel was dedicated to her in Glasgow, near the modern St Enoch's Square – the name St Enoch is said to be a corruption of St Thenaw; naturally her bones rested in her chapel.

Mungo himself came to Glasgow on the instruction of an angel. He built a church on the banks of the Molendinar burn where the Cathedral now stands. He was visited there by St Columba who composed a Latin hymn in celebration of the meeting. Temporarily driven out from the city by the hostility of a pagan king, he spent some years in Wales and founded the bishopric which bears the name of his disciple St Asaph. He then returned to Glasgow to be greeted by an enthusiastic crowd. They were so numerous indeed that the future saint was soon hidden from general view. However, he began to preach and, as he did so, the earth on which he stood was raised up to form a hill, so that all could see and hear him. This tradition is commemorated in the city's motto: 'Let Glasgow Flourish by the Preaching of the Word'.

It was not the only miracle associated with the saint, who died at a great age, as saints tend to do unless they are martyred or die in adolescence, and was buried in the little wooden church which he had founded. Among his miracles are those which are commemorated in the arms of the city of Glasgow; they show a tree, with a bird perched on its branches; on one side is a salmon, with a ring in its mouth; on the other a bell.

The tree recalls a miracle which Mungo performed at Culross. The lamps of the monastery had all gone out, and so Mungo took the frozen branch of a hazel, made the sign of the cross over it; instantly it burst into flame.

The bird is a pet robin belonging to his master St Serf. It was killed accidentally, indeed torn to pieces, by some of his disciples, whereupon Mungo restored it to life.

The salmon commemorates an equally remarkable story. A certain queen lost a ring which her husband had given her. He suspected that she had given it to her lover and was about to put her to death. The lady had the good sense to apply to Mungo, who requested that the first fish to be caught in the Clyde should be brought to him. When this was done, the ring was discovered in its mouth.

The bell was not miraculous. It was brought by Mungo from Rome, and was to be preserved in Glasgow at least till the Reformation. It was the custom to toll it to announce a death and call the citizens to pray for the soul of the departed.

These emblems appear in the seals of the pre-Reformation Bishops of Glasgow as early as the twelfth century, no doubt as a result of an earlier Life of the saint, apparently composed between 1147 and 1164, which now survives only in fragments. At the beginning of the fourteenth century they were transferred to the common seal of the city.

It is easy to cast doubt on these miracles, indeed on everything connected with Mungo, except perhaps his very existence. But it is also pointless. We know little that is authentic about him, for the two Lives were written more than five hundred years after his death. No doubt some of what they say is invention, deeds expected of saints. Some will be adaptation, in order to connect Mungo with figures such as King Lot who play a part in the Arthurian cycle. But much is likely to be the codification of oral tradition.

In a sense it doesn't matter. The reality of Mungo is testified by the reality of Glasgow, just as the chief witness to the existence of Romulus is the fact of the city of Rome and its history. More precisely, the reality of Mungo is confirmed by the reality of the Christian tradition of Glasgow. Nothing physical remains, though Mungo's burial place reputedly was the Cathedral; a lamp burns over his grave. Yet, if that is all, and even that not certain, if Mungo himself would recognise nothing in Glasgow today, the city remains his spiritual legacy.

Even his two names are significant, particularly the Glasgow preference for Mungo rather than Kentigern. The latter means 'noble lord', the former 'dear one'. Glasgow has scarcely ever been a city where noble lords played much part, just as it was never fortified, never a military stronghold. But it has always been a city which valued the claims of affection highly, a warm, friendly, even sentimental place. It is appropriate that it should call its saint by his intimate name, rather than by his resounding one.

Mungo is not the only saint associated with the early days of Glasgow, for Old Govan Parish Church across the river from the Cathedral stands on the site of a church reputedly built by St Constantine in the seventh century. However, Govan, being on the other side of the Clyde, was for long not part of Glasgow proper, and Glasgow remains correctly St Mungo's city.

It was the Church that made it, though for long there was open country between the ecclesiastical settlement on the Molendinar and the little salmon-fishing village on the Clyde. The history of Glasgow, as distinct from legend, may be dated from 1115 when the king's brother David, the future David I, whom James I would describe as 'a sair saint for the crown', established, or re-established, the episcopal see. David, himself the son of a saint, Queen Margaret, the wife of Malcolm Canmore, was the greatest royal benefactor of the Church in Scotland. Even before his accession to the throne, he was lord of most of Scotland south of the Forth, and as a result of his marriage to Matilda, daughter of Earl Waltheof of Northumberland, lord of the northern counties of modern England as well. Two years earlier he had established a monastery of reformed Benedictines at Selkirk, and endowed them with large estates both in Scotland and in his other English earldom of Huntingdon. In 1126, acting on the advice of his chancellor John, whom he had made the first Bishop of Glasgow, he transferred this abbey to Kelso and dedicated it to the Virgin and St John the Evangelist. Its first abbot was one Herbert who would succeed John as Bishop of Glasgow. His successor was Joceline, Abbot of Melrose, also founded and endowed by David. Meanwhile in 1136 a new stone cathedral, replacing the old wooden structure, was consecrated in Glasgow. The king endowed it with the lands of Partick and restored to it other possessions which the old church had apparently lost.

Glasgow, therefore, owes more to David I than to any other monarch. He may fairly be called the heir to St Mungo. There was no bishop then in Edinburgh, and Glasgow was the only bishopric south of the Forth except Galloway. Its bishop therefore held lands, and exerted influence, through-out the south of Scotland. Eventually, not long before the Reformation, during the pontificate of the Borgia Pope, Alexander VI, a bull was obtained elevating the see of Glasgow to an archbishopric, despite bitter opposition from Shevez, Archbishop of St Andrews, who rightly considered that this detracted from his importance as Primate of Scotland. Nevertheless, it was done, and Robert Blacader became first Archbishop of Glasgow in 1492; the bishops of Galloway, Argyll, and the Isles were made his suffragans. Glasgow had therefore become the second ecclesiastical city in Scotland.

Only in the religious sphere was it a great place. It had not even been a burgh till 1180 when William the Lion granted it a charter, but as a dependent burgh, holding from the bishop, not as a royal burgh, though that status was soon held by neighbouring towns: Dumbarton, Renfrew and Rutherglen. It did not assume that rank definitively till 1611, though in

1450 the bishop had obtained from James III a charter erecting all his patrimony into a regality, and from that date the chief magistrate of the city was called the Lord Provost.

The year 1451 saw the foundation of the University, the second oldest in Scotland, junior only to St Andrews. Authority for its establishment was first obtained by Bishop Turnbull from Pope Nicholas V, and this was confirmed by royal charter in 1453. It was first situated within the Cathedral, then in a house in Rottenrow, a street which now barely exists, but which was then inhabited by clerics. A little later it moved to a site down the High Street where it remained till the middle of the nineteenth century. When it moved, the railway built a goods station in its place, itself now being redeveloped. The University is not as old as the Glasgow Grammar School, later the High School of Glasgow, which had been established in the Cathedral precincts in the fourteenth century, and possibly earlier. The two oldest educational establishments in Glasgow are therefore children of the Church.

The bishops dominated the medieval city. Till the Reformation they appointed the magistrates. Apart from its ecclesiastical connection, the city was little more than a local market-town. It consisted of one main street running from the Cathedral down to Glasgow Cross, and thence, irregularly, to the bridge across the Clyde; the last part of it was already called the Briggait, or Bridgegait, gait or gate being the old Scots term for a walk or way. Half a dozen small streets led off this main one. The two most important were the Gallowgate which led east across the Molendinar burn to the town moor, and St Thenaw's Gate. The Church of St Mungo-in-the Fields stood north of the Gallowgate, surrounded by a cemetery and with trees reputedly planted by the saint himself. Like any medieval city Glasgow was full of churches, chapels and other religious foundations. There was a Dominican priory on the east side of the High Street near the future site of the University and the Gothic Dominican church stood there from 1246 to 1670. There were two chapels in St Thenaw's Gate, besides one dedicated to St Thenaw herself. One was Our Lady's Chapel, the other consecrated to St Thomas à Becket. In the same street was a collegiate church dedicated to the Virgin and St Anne, her mother, endowed for a provost, eight canons and three choristers. It stood there till 1793 when it was destroyed by fire and replaced by the Tron Kirk, now a theatre.

But the greatest church, and the reason for Glasgow's fame, was the Cathedral. It is unique in Scotland, the only medieval cathedral to have survived the ravages of war and the pious zeal of the Reformers. The survival is not complete. The stained glass and images of the medieval church fell victim to the Reformers' hatred of idolatry. Moreover, as in other cathedrals, most of the monuments and memorials belong to recent centuries. It has been a Protestant church now for more than four hundred years, and Protestant martyrs are commemorated. Yet even the interior retains much that is old. The Quire Screen, or Pulpitum, dating from about 1500, is the only one left in a Scottish secular church from pre-Reformation times. The two altar platforms were added in 1503 by Archbishop Blacader, whose coat of arms they bear. The same Archbishop built the beautiful Blacader Aisle. Superficially that is almost all. The glass is modern, and it replaces nineteenth-century glass, made in Munich; this is preserved in the Lower, or Laigh, Church, and offers an interesting and pleasing example of German Pre-Raphaelite art. There is some old carving – a fifteenth-century Green Man with leaves issuing from his mouth, for instance – but most of the carving, like the glass, offended the reforming spirit.

And yet the Cathedral does not feel like the Presbyterian church it has now been for four centuries. This is most apparent when you descend to the Laigh Church. (It is not a crypt, since it is above ground level, on account of the way the ground falls away abruptly to the valley of the Molendinar.) At its east end are five little chapels, most of which have recently been consecrated to a particular function. So there is the chapel of St Nicholas, dedicated to the children of the Cathedral in 1969; the chapel of St Andrew, dedicated in 1961 'as a place of prayer and meditation for members of the nursing profession'; the chapel of St Peter and St Paul, the ancient burial ground of the Orrs of Broomfield; the chapel of St John the Evangelist with St Mungo's Well; and the Chapel and Tomb of St Mungo himself.

Stand contemplating these little chapels, or pray there a moment, and it is as if the spirit of medieval Christianity, enshrined in the great Cathedral, has conquered the rational and reductive faith of the Reformers. They despised and loathed the Roman idea that saints could serve as intermediaries between man and God. They regarded the Catholic reverence for the Virgin Mary as an abomination; and yet the Mother of Jesus and the Saints have triumphed. The Cathedral has absorbed the Reformers, and, though not forgetting to do honour to them, has corrected their errors. Some people, with imagination, may linger in Glasgow Cathedral sensing what Scotland lost, perhaps, as a result of the breach with Rome. It is impossible in this church to forget that Scotland was a Catholic country longer than it has been a Protestant one.

The last four Catholic archbishops of Glasgow were all exercised by the matter of heresy as the authority of the historic church was questioned. Blacader himself had persecuted the remnants of Wyclif's proto-Protestant movement, Lollardry. Then in 1487 one James Resby was burnt in Glasgow for affirming that the Pope was not the 'Vicar of Christ' and for claiming that a man of wicked life should not be Pope; that would have been difficult to arrange in Renaissance Rome, for it was only a few years since Alexander VI, the patron of Archbishop Blacader, had aspired to make the Papacy hereditary. Blacader's successor but one, James Dunbar, though described as of mild disposition, nevertheless presided over the burning of James Russell, a dissident Franciscan friar, and an Ayrshire boy of eighteen, John Kennedy. It is not surprising that the magnificent tomb he constructed for himself did not survive the Reformers' zeal.

The last Catholic archbishop was James Beaton, a nephew of the more famous David Beaton of St Andrews. He went into exile in France in 1560. Queen Mary made him her ambassador there, and James VI, who also found him useful as a diplomat despite religious differences, obtained for him, by special Act of Parliament in 1598, the revenues of the see from which he had been forced to flee. He died in 1603, the year of the Union of the Crowns, at the age of eighty-six.

On his departure from Glasgow he had piously removed the relics, records, charters and much of the plate from his cathedral. Among the relics were many objects of interest. There was, as befitted any respect-worthy cathedral, a portion of the True Cross; indeed there were several. But there were also silver caskets guarding objects of great interest and devotion: the skin of St Bartholomew the Apostle, the hair of the Blessed Virgin, part of her girdle, scourges used by St Mungo and by St Thomas of Canterbury. There was a small saffron-coloured phial containing fluid which formerly flowed from the tomb of St Mungo, and there was a phial of crystal which purportedly held the milk of the Blessed Virgin and a part, presumably small, of the manger of Christ.

The archbishop guarded these relics throughout his time in France and left them in his will to the Scots College in Paris which he had effectively re-established. But he also requested that everything he had brought from Glasgow should be restored to his Cathedral, as soon as the inhabitants of the city should return to the True Church.

On 12 August 1560 the Lords of the Congregation in Edinburgh dispatched instructions throughout the kingdom:

To Our Traist Friendis,
Traist Friends, after maist hearty commendacion, we pray you fail not to pass incontinent to the kirk and tak down the hail images thereof, and bring furth the kirk-zyard, and burn thaym openly. And sicklyke cast-down the alteris, and purge the kirk of all kynd of monuments of idolatrye. And this ze fail not

11

to do, as ze will do us singular emplesur, and so committis you to the protection of God.

The letter was signed by the Earls of Moray and Argyll and Lord Ruthven. Glasgow did not fail to suffer, and, when he heard of it, Archbishop Beaton must have commended himself for his prudence in removing the Virgin's milk and Christ's manger which could hardly have been expected to survive the assault.

Zeal was not satisfied, however. Fourteen years later an act was passed by the Estates authorising the demolition of churches which still bore the taint of Rome. Andrew Melville, Principal of the University of Glasgow, newly appointed on his return from Geneva, approved whole-heartedly. He had already asked the magistrates to pull down the Cathedral, and build three new, and chaster, churches from its stones. On receipt of this letter from the Protestant lords, the magistrates yielded to his requests. The drum was sounded to call labourers to the Holy Work. The craft guilds, however, who were proud of their Cathedral on which so many of their former members had been employed, moved to prevent Melville. Indeed, they made it clear to him that if a single stone was pulled down, he would soon find himself under it. In these circumstances he wisely abandoned his plan, not before the magistrates had had to intervene to protect him from the crowd's anger.

Melville and the ministers protested to Edinburgh, and the leaders of the guilds were summoned before the Council there for examination. The young James VI, however, already conscious of the challenge which the presumptions of the kirk's ministers posed to the authority of the crown, approved the defence of the Cathedral. Too many churches, he said, had already been destroyed, and he was not prepared to tolerate more abuses of that kind. This thwarting of Melville's wishes adds something to the celebrated later exchange between king and minister, when Melville informed James that there were two kingdoms in Scotland, one being that of Christ Jesus, whose kingdom was the Kirk, in which kingdom James 'was not a king, nor a lord, but a member'; 'nought', as he said, 'but 'God's silly vassal'.

Melville comes badly out of the Cathedral episode. It shows him as an iconoclast without reverence for the achievement of past centuries. By contrast, his few years as Principal of the University of Glasgow were notable for intelligent reform. The leading Reformers were men of wide education: John Knox had studied at St Andrews under the great humanist historian John Major; George Buchanan was recognised as one of the foremost intellectuals of Europe; and Melville had studied at the universities of St Andrews, Paris, Poitiers and Geneva. It is not surprising that such men were in favour of university reform. Melville was only Principal of the University of Glasgow for five years before he moved on to St Andrews. It was long enough to allow him to introduce a new curriculum and to reform the teaching system. Previously a regent had been responsible for the complete education of a class, taking it through the whole course of study. Melville, drawing on his continental experience, introduced specialist teachers, each responsible for his own particular branch of study. His reforms were embodied in a new charter for the University, granted by the Regent Morton in 1577, which also put its finances on a more secure basis.

Despite their defence of the Cathedral, the citizens had embraced the Reformation with enthusiasm. It did not languish. Glasgow would become known as a zealously Protestant and Presbyterian city, always hostile to the attempts of the Stewart kings to re-establish royal control over the Church. During the brief flurry of 1568, when Queen Mary had escaped from Loch Leven, and hoped to regain power with the help of the Hamiltons and other noble families, the Glasgow citizens staunchly supported the Regent Moray, the city's bakers making 'extraordinary exertions' to supply his army with bread. As a result the incorporation of bakers was granted the archbishop's flour-mill at Partick which had passed to the Crown at the Reformation; thus was their pious zeal rewarded.

In those days indeed there was good reason to believe in Glasgow that God approved the Reformation performed in his name. There was, for instance, the case of the Stewarts of Minto. This once great family had a close relationship with the Cathedral and indeed their family memorial is one of the few to survive the Reformation; a more recent plaque, however, records that the family's fame rests in having supplied Charles II with one of his mistresses, Frances Stewart, who long resisted his advances, was made Duchess of Richmond and posed as the model for Britannia.

The family's connection with the Cathedral was not always happy. Sir Matthew Stewart of Minto was Lord Provost of Glasgow in 1581 when James VI made his first attempt to restore episcopacy in Scotland. James appointed Robert Montgomery Archbishop of Glasgow. The citizens objected, and on the day of Montgomery's induction he found the pulpit occupied by a Presbyterian minister called Howie. The Lord Provost was determined that the King should be obeyed. He ordered Howie out of the pulpit. Howie refused to leave. Sir Matthew therefore removed him by force. In the struggle the minister lost a few teeth and part of his beard. He had the last word, however, cursing the Lord Provost and calling down the judgement of God on him and his family: within a few generations the

13

Stewarts were reduced to beggary.

The enthusiasm for the Presbyterian faith was not tempered in Glasgow by the enthusiasm with which the ministers of the kirk embarked on policies of moral and social control. They were quick to command attendance at church, with fines levied on those absent, and to forbid the transaction of any business during 'the hour of the sermon' even on weekdays. The celebration of Christmas was also forbidden; in 1582 five people were ordered to make a public display of repentance for having 'observed the superstitious day called Yuil'; moreover, 'the baxters' (bakers) were 'to be inquired at, to whom they baked Yuil bread'. Chastity was a public concern. For a single breach, male servants were to be fined thirty pounds Scots, or else serve eight days in prison, on a diet of bread and water, 'thereafter to be put in the jougs' (iron neck-ring). Those of a higher social rank might get off more lightly. In 1608 the Laird of Minto, again, was let off with a reprimand 'on account of his age and the position he held in the town'. Whores, however, could expect rougher treatment: they were to be carted through the town – that is, dragged at the tail of a cart – ducked in the Clyde and stood in the stocks. Adulterers could expect similar punishment; a pulley was fixed on the bridge over the Clyde to facilitate ducking. A later edict from the kirk session, delivered in 1643 – a time of intense religious excitement on account of the Civil Wars – ordered that adulterers should be whipped during, but presumably not throughout, their three hours in the stocks.

None of this severity was unique to Glasgow, to Scotland or even to Presbyterianism. Archbishop Hamilton, the last Scottish primate before the Reformation, had issued a Catechism in 1552 which laid equal emphasis on Sabbath observance and strict morality. If the Kirk Session of Glasgow persecuted harlots, so did the Counter-Reformation Pope Pius V, who issued an edict expelling all prostitutes from Rome unless they married or entered a convent. This was not successful, any more than the Glasgow edicts were, though the Pope did manage to confine them to a special quarter or ghetto. This same Pope yielded nothing to Glasgow in his hostility to adulterers; indeed he tried to impose the death penalty. The moral austerity of the Kirk Session of Glasgow belonged to the age rather than the city.

One other aspect is worth comment. This was the enthusiasm with which the ministers and elders of the Kirk set themselves to extinguishing any flickering embers of popery: 2250 citizens signed the Negative Confession of Faith of 1581 which specifically repudiated papal claims. It may be assumed that the number did not include Sir Bartholomew Simpson in whose chamber in 1588 'was yesterday found certain boards and pictures, being the monuments of idolatry'; he was commanded 'to pass immediately thereafter with them to the cross and set the same on fire'. Four years later a certain Mrs Robertson, a widow, confessed that she had sinned against God and his kirk by keeping 'pictures of the Virgin Mary and the babe Jesus, as well as mass-clouts, mass-books and priests' bonnets'. She had to burn them; what's more she was required to do so 'at the cross, in a fire made at her own expense'.

Glasgow Cathedral was to be the scene in 1639 of the great General Assembly of the Kirk which confirmed the National Covenant signed in Greyfriars Churchyard in Edinburgh in February 1638, and which gave the signal for the disintegration of Charles I's authority that was to end, ten years later, in his execution. Probably no other meeting held in the city has had greater political consequence.

The quarrel between Charles and Scotland ostensibly concerned the matter of Church Government; Charles wanted bishops because, apart from any question of doctrine, he believed that only through episcopacy could the king control the Church and manage public opinion. The Scots rejected bishops partly for scriptural reasons, partly because they were incompatible with the democratic nature of Calvinism, and partly, in the case of the nobility and the lairds, because they resented Charles I's attempt, in the Act of Revocation of 1625, to recover as much as he could of the old church property which had passed into their hands.

The signing of the National Covenant had given expression to opposition which had been developing for a dozen years. The meeting of the Assembly, a lawful body, since it was summoned by the king, was awaited with great excitement in Glasgow. The excitement was not entirely political. Those with accommodation to let hoped to do well out of the influx of delegates. There were 240 of these, 142 being ministers, the rest laymen, elders appointed by presbyteries. The total number of visitors was much greater, for the Privy Council also attended, and there were numerous assessors. Many were accompanied by servants, and though the King's Commissioner, the Marquess of Hamilton, issued a proclamation banning the presence of retainers and the bearing of arms, this was disregarded.

The Town Council had prepared for the influx. More than a month before the Assembly was due to meet they had ordered 'that no burgess or inhabitant within this burgh shall set, or promise to set, for rent or otherwise, to give to any friend, any house, chamber or stable, unless they first acquaint them [the magistrates] therwith, that the provost, bailies and council may give a licence thereto, to the end that everyone may be lodged according to their quality and ability in this city, under the pain of £100, and imprisonment of their persons during the magistrates' will ...; and also, that no inhabitant expect more rent for the house, chambers, beds and stables, than shall be appointed by the said provost, bailies and council ...'

It is a delusion to suppose that minute regulation is a disease only of the modern bureaucratic state. The Revd Robert Baillie, a future Principal of the University of Glasgow, noted the success of this exercise in price-fixing. 'The town expected, and provided for, huge multitudes of people, and put on their beds and houses excessive prices; but the diligence of the magistrates, and the vacancy of many rooms, quickly moderated that excess.' He noted that Glasgow could 'lodge easily at once, council, session, parliament and general assembly, if need would require'; and so leaves it in doubt whether prices were actually controlled by the council's regulatory activity or by the operation of market forces.

The crowd on the first day of the Assembly was so great that the town guard had difficulty in opening a way for the members to reach their seats. Many of the crowd were retainers of the nobility and gentry, but Baillie, who had himself been in favour of episcopacy as recently as the previous year and who came from a landed family, was highly critical of the Glasgow populace: 'It is here alone,' he thought, 'where we might learn from Canterbury, yea, from the Pope, from the Turks, or pagans, modesty and manners ... Our rascals without shame, in great numbers, made such a din and clamour in the house of the true God, that if they minded to use the like behaviour in my own chambers, I could not be content till they were down the stair.'

Nevertheless, more adroit politicans than Baillie saw that the excited mood of the people contributed towards the expectation and uncertainty which helped to undermine the confidence of the King's Commissioner. Hamilton was perturbed by what his biographer Bishop Burnet called 'the greatest confluence of people that perhaps ever met in these parts of Europe at an assembly'. In less than a week he pronounced its dissolution. But the Assembly continued to sit. It had ceased to exist at law; but it continued there in fact. One minister declared that 'they had a better master, Christ the King of Kings, to serve ... and therefore he moved that, having this in their eye, they might sit still and do their Master's work faithfully ...' That work would see episcopacy swept aside, and the authority of the king rejected in reality, though not altogether in form. It was the outbreak of national revolution.

Glasgow, that pacific city, played little active part in the Civil Wars of the next decade though it was consistently to the fore, second only to Edinburgh, in its financial contribution to the Covenanting cause. It also contributed some 150 men at the town's expense to the Bishops' Wars of 1639–40; yet, though fiercely Covenanting, responded prudently four years later to the change of fortune represented by the Marquess of Montrose's campaign of 1644–5. The news of his victory at Kilsyth alarmed the magistrates, for Kilsyth is only twelve miles from the city. They sent a message of congratulation, offered £500 in English money, praying that the city should escape a sack. Montrose complied. He had himself been a Covenanter and attended the great Assembly in Glasgow; he had no wish for further violence and indeed saw the necessity of national reconciliation. The Lord Provost and bailies gave a dinner for him and his officers, and he hanged some of his own men who had disobeyed orders and looted some shops in the Gallowgate and Saltmarket. He departed within a few days, either because of rumours of plague or because he saw that Glasgow might provide too severe a temptation for the discipline of his Irish and Highland soldiers. The city was relieved.

Montrose's defeat at Philiphaugh four weeks later imposed a new strain on Glasgow, however, for it now suffered for its earlier prudence; the Covenanting General, David Leslie, borrowing a large sum from the city as interest, he said, for the entertainment offered Montrose.

The Marquess had summoned a Parliament to meet in Glasgow; instead a Court of Law passed sentence on those who had fought in his army and been taken prisoner. Three were executed at Glasgow Cross by the end of the month, one a boy of eighteen – 'a lovely young youth,' said the Glasgow bailie who presided at his execution. 'The wark gaes merrily on,' observed an approving minister of religion.

It continued to do so, violence breeding violence. Charles I surrendered to the Scots, was handed over to the English army, and sought new allies among those alarmed that the English Revolution now threatened their interests. He found some in Scotland. The Engagement was signed in 1648, binding Royalists and some former Covenanters together. Levees of troops, money and provisions were commanded. Glasgow declined to respond. The Lord Provost and bailies were imprisoned, and deprived of office by an Act of the Scottish Parliament. When they were released, they found soldiers billeted on them. Robert Baillie, now Principal of the University, observed that Montrose had cost the city less.

In London, King Charles I was executed in 1649. The Scots proclaimed his son Charles II, and then compelled him to sign the Covenant. Cromwell invaded Scotland, defeated the Scottish army at Dunbar, advanced on

Edinburgh and then proceeded to Glasgow, where he took up lodgings in the Saltmarket. He sent for the Revd Patrick Gillespie, minister of the Outer High Church, who, having spoken and prayed with the General, assured the people that 'surely he must be one of the elect'. Cromwell remained grateful to the minister who had given such a good opinion of him to the citizens; two years later he made Gillespie Principal of the University in succession to Robert Baillie. In 1655 Gillespie went to London and returned with a grant for his college of the greater part of the revenues of the old See of Galloway.

The Cromwellian occupation was generally beneficial rather than harmful to the city. For the first time, though briefly, its merchants were offered the chance to trade freely with England and English colonies. The experience so gained and contacts made would enable them to pursue a small-scale, though illegal, trade with the West Indies and the Americas after the Restoration when Scottish merchants had again been excluded from the English colonial trade.

The Restoration gave a new twist to the politics of faction and religion. Episcopacy was restored again to the great dissatisfaction of Glasgow and the West. The 'Killing Time' in the 1680s is a period of Scottish history much distorted by partisan writers. The severity of the Government is unquestioned; advocates for the persecuted Covenanters long obscured the revolutionary purpose of their party, who were fighting not simply for liberty of conscience but for the right to impose their conscience upon others. Nevertheless there is generally some truth in historical mythology; at the very least, if it does not accurately represent what happened, it forms the mind of succeeding generations. A memorial in Glasgow Cathedral bears witness to the moral triumph of the Covenanters:

Robert Burton   John Hart   Robert Scot   Matthew Patoun
John Richmond   Archibald Stewart   James Winning   John Main
who suffered at the Cross of Glasgow for their testimony to the Covenants
and work of reformation because they durst not own the authority of the
then tyrants destroying the same, betwixt 1666 and 1688.

Years sixty-six and eighty-four
Did send their souls home with glore
Whose bodies here interred ly
Then sacrificed to tyranny;
To covenants and reformation
'Cause they adhered in their station
These nine, with others in their yard
Whose heads and bodies were not spar'd,

Their testimonies, foes, to bury,
Caus'd beat the drums then in great fury,
They'll know at Resurrection day
To murder saints was no sweet play ...

The verse is execrable, the sentiments sincere. It was no wonder that when the Revolution broke out in 1688, the Cathedral was attacked by a mob of Presbyterians joined by some of the 'suffering and persecuted brethren of the western hills'. It was, says Macaulay, 'a Sunday; but to rabble a congregation of prelatists was held to be a work of necessity and mercy. The worshippers were dispersed, beaten and pelted with snowballs.' The Lord Provost, Walter Gibson, who was an Episcopalian, had a report prepared for the Privy Council; but his time was past. The city and Cathedral were soon in the hands of his enemies, and the 'suffering saints' avenged.

Questions of religion, inseparable from questions of politics, agitated people throughout the seventeenth century. Yet the daily life of a commercial city continued in parallel. Glasgow, like other cities, was still organised on lines common to all urban settlements since the High Middle Ages. A burgh was a privileged community, granted certain rights or liberties by charter, and jealous to safeguard them. Only burgesses might carry on any kind of retail trade within the burgh limits. The association of burgesses or merchant guild protected its privileges and regulated admission to their enjoyment. Entry to the guild required apprenticeship to a merchant in the first instance, and then payment of a fee to the corporation. Sons of burgesses and those able to marry daughters of burgesses were favoured; in Glasgow aspirants who possessed neither of these qualifications had to wait two years longer, and pay a higher entry-fee. On the whole, these merchants lived modestly. Few of them seem to have aspired to own estates beyond the town; an ambitious man such as the Lord Provost, Walter Gibson, who commissioned Sir William Bruce, the architect employed by Charles II at Holyroodhouse, to build him a splendid town house, was rare.

Below the merchant guild came the 'incorporated trades' who were also burgesses. There were fourteen of these in Glasgow, each headed by an elected deacon. The purpose of the craft guilds was the same as that of the merchant guild; they were protective associations. T. C. Smout observes:

Characteristically, when the blacksmiths, goldsmiths, lorimers, saddlers, bucklemakers and other metal workers of Glasgow petitioned in 1536 for permission to set up an 'Incorporation of Hammermen' they grounded their

19

application on the 'great hurt and damage' suffered by other honest burgesses from the work of unqualified men, and made their first rule that no one should be allowed to set up a metalware booth in the town unless he was an admitted member of the craft examined and found qualified to work by three of the best masters.

Theoretically these guilds established standards of production. In fact, the quality of their work often seems to have been low, partly perhaps because the richer classes in Scotland preferred to buy goods of foreign manufacture so that local producers were catering for customers with little disposable income. This was a vicious circle out of which it was hard to break, especially since the organisation of the crafts discouraged innovation and competition within the city.

Together the merchant guild and the craft guilds made up perhaps 10 per cent of the population of a city such as Glasgow. In 1604 when the population was between 7000 and 8000 the fourteen crafts had 361 members and the merchant guild 213. Considering the long period of apprenticeship required, this represents quite a high figure. In some guilds the numbers of apprentices that a master could take on was limited; it was necessary to restrict production to secure a sufficiently high standard of living for guild members.

The largest guild in Glasgow in 1604 was the Incorporation of Tailors with sixty-five members. Then followed in descending order: maltsters and shoemakers (cordiners), weavers, hammer-men, bakers, coopers, skinners, wrights, fleshers, masons, bonnet-makers, dyers and surgeons. The composition of the list emphasises the largely domestic nature of the economy.

Only merchants and craftsmen could be burgesses. All the rest possessed neither rights nor privileges, though these were generally granted by the town council to professional men such as lawyers and ministers. Other inhabitants of the city were 'unfreemen': journeymen, casual labourers, servants, most of whom were female. There were those who kept cows in the city and sold milk and butter, and those licensed to sell ale. The council kept a close eye on them. In 1661, for example, when one William Watson, a candle-maker and notorious drunkard, 'always a bad example to all vicious livers', was arrested 'at two or three hours of the morning', breaking the face of the guard 'to the effusion of his blood', the ale-seller in whose house this all happened, one James Hamilton, lost his licence. He and his wife, the council recorded, 'keipis ane verie lewd hous, and will not amend, though oft admonished'. Theirs was a judgement which would be repeated time and again throughout the city's history.

The Revolution of 1688–9 signalled the end of Scotland's age of violent religious dissension. Sectarian disputes and acrimony continued and have scarcely ceased, but after the Revolution men no longer murdered and persecuted in the name of true religion. A form of church government satisfactory to the majority of Scots, and no longer obnoxious to the monarchy, was established. Scotland stood on the verge of an age when energies were diverted from politico-religious controversy to the pursuit of wealth, when Jehovah seemed to be supplanted by Mercury.

The first intimation of this new interest was disastrous. This was the Darien Scheme, promoted by William Paterson, a Dumfriesshire man and the founder of the Bank of England. The scheme was seductive in its simplicity, chimerical in its disregard for political realities. Its purpose was to plant a Scottish colony on the isthmus of Darien in Panama, which would serve as an entrepôt for the Atlantic and Pacific trades. The logic was impeccable, if only physical geography was to be considered; it foundered on the facts of political geography: on the refusal of Spain to allow Scottish colonists to establish themselves within their Spanish Empire and on the opposition of the English East India Company, which declined to surrender its monopoly of trade with the East.

Scotland, however, was inflamed by the prospect of unprecedented wealth. The Company of Scotland Trading to Africa and the Indies was established by Act of Parliament in 1695. Paterson's original intention was that half the Company's capital should be subscribed in London and the Netherlands; he had been encouraged to believe this possible by English merchants who were themselves anxious to break the East India Company's monopoly. That company was too strong, however. It made representations at Court, which were sufficient to persuade the Dutch King William III and dissuade any prospective investors. It was left to Scotland, therefore, to finance the enterprise out of the country's own scanty resources. The response was astonishing; it was estimated that half the circulating wealth of the nation was invested in Darien stock.

Glasgow was enthusiastic for the scheme. Trade with England and Ulster had developed in the seventeenth century, but now for the first time in history it seemed as if the currents of trade might substantially favour the city. Geography had made the east coast ports the natural centres for European commerce; now the New World could be called into being to redress the balance of wealth in Scotland. The citizens subscribed with enthusiasm; many embarked as prospective colonists and traders on the four expeditions that set out in 1698 and 1699 for the colony which was to be Scotland's El Dorado. The last of these sailed from Rothesay Bay with

1200 emigrants, who included the last representative of the once-great Stewarts of Minto.

It was natural that Glasgow should be optimistic; the city had already experienced some benefits from its illicit Atlantic trade. The shock of failure was therefore in proportion to the weight of expectation. The financial loss was appalling; the moral shock correspondingly great. Glasgow's merchants would possess no ships of their own for almost twenty years after the collapse of the Company of Scotland Trading to Africa and the Indies.

That collapse, and the implications for the future if England and Scotland continued to pursue antagonistic trading policies, combined with uncertainty about the succession to the throne to turn minds to the possibility of a full union between the two countries. Within a year or two of Queen Anne's accession in 1702 it seemed to many that the choice lay between separation and incorporation; little support was found for the proposal of Federal Union advanced by Andrew Fletcher of Saltoun, then the most acute political thinker in Scotland.

Scotland was deeply divided. There was a clear cleavage between those in the political class who could see the advantages of political security and economic expansion which the Union offered, and the ordinary people who saw only the shame entailed in the loss of that independence which Scotland had defended for centuries. But the divisions were not as simple as that. Within the propertied classes were Jacobites who saw in the Union the extinction of their hope that the Stewarts would be recalled to the throne and that they themselves would resume political power in Scotland, and within the class of those who resented the prospective loss of independence there were craftsmen who feared that, for them, the economic consequence of Union would be greater exposure to English competition.

This feeling was powerful in Glasgow, where hostility to the Union was intense. The magistrates were so alarmed by the mood of the city that in October 1707, after the publication of the Articles of the proposed Treaty, they issued a proclamation forbidding any assembly of more than three people after sunset. It was not effective. The people were not lacking in spiritual encouragement. The Commission of the General Assembly of the Church of Scotland decreed a fast-day to implore Divine deliverance from the impending calamity of Union. The minister of the Tron Kirk, the Revd James Clark, took as his text on the fast-day Ezra 8:21: 'And I proclaimed a fast there at the river of Ahava, that we might afflict ourselves before our God, to seek of him a right way for us and for our little ones, and for all our substance.' He warned them that prayer, though a duty, might be insufficient in itself: 'Wherefore, up and be valiant for the city of our God.'

The people hurried to obey. They stormed the Lord Provost's house, broke his windows and removed twenty-five muskets. Their victim removed himself to Edinburgh. While he was out of the city, an address against the Union was circulated and signed by as many as could write their name. It was then sent to the Parliament in Edinburgh by the Lord Dean of Guild, the deacon of the tailors and the deacon of the shoemakers (two trades, incidentally, which might be expected to suffer from English competition). The city calmed down, the Lord Provost returned, only to encounter fresh disturbances. A tobacco-spinner named Parker had been arrested for offering for sale one of the muskets taken from the Lord Provost's house. He was confined in the Tolbooth, where he was visited by numerous sympathisers. The chief of these was an ex-soldier called Finlay, known as a Jacobite and described as 'a loose sort of fellow... who followed no employ, but his mother kept a little change-house at the remotest part of the town, on the Edinburgh side'. Anxious to placate the people and avoid further disturbances, the Lord Provost had Parker released on signing a bond, as security for good behaviour. Finlay and his friends, however, sensing the mood, demanded that the bond should be surrendered to them. Pursuing their policy of appeasement, the Lord Provost and bailies agreed to this also. Their prudence or weakness was ill rewarded. Daniel Defoe, in his *History of the Union*, drawing on the evidence of eyewitnesses, gives a vivid account of what followed:

The provost, not imagining any danger, having granted their request, comes innocently out of the tolbooth, and went toward his own house; the rabble gathered immediately about him, thrusting and abusing him, and not with villainous language only, but with stones and dirt and such like thrown at him. He would have made to his own house, but the multitude increasing, and growing furious, he took sanctuary in a house, and running up a staircase lost the rabble for some time – they pursuing him into a wrong house [a distinct dwelling within a tenement]; however, they searched every apartment to the top of the stair, and came into the very room where he was. But the same hand that smote the men of Sodom with blindness, when they would have rabbled the angels, protected him from this many-headed monster, and so blinded them that they could not find him. It is the opinion of many of the soberest and most judicious of the citizens, that if they had found him, their fury was at that time so past all government that they would have murdered him, and that in a manner barbarous enough; and if they had, as we say of a bull-dog, once but tasted blood, who knows where they would have ended. The provost was hid in a bed, which folded up against the wall, and which they never thought of taking down; having escaped this imminent danger he was conveyed out of town the next day by his friends, and went for the second time to Edinburgh. The rabble were now fully masters of the town. They ranged the streets and did what they pleased. No magistrate durst show his face to them. They challenged people, as they walked the streets, with this question – 'Are you for the Union?'; and no man durst own it but at their extremest hazard.

The insurgents, or loyal opposition, were in control of the city for a fortnight. At one point Finlay even set out with forty or fifty men, for Edinburgh, proclaiming his intention of dismissing the Parliament and so averting the Union. The intention was to join a rendezvous of those opposed to the Union on the Hamilton Estates (now Strathclyde Park). Gathering no support on the way, discovering even that the main part of his force refused to leave Glasgow, his courage or confidence evaporated by the time he reached Kilsyth, and so he slipped back to Glasgow. Meanwhile the Government in Edinburgh sent a force of dragoons and horse grenadiers, under Colonel Campbell, an uncle of the Duke of Argyll. This brought the rioters to their senses. They gave up their stolen weapons to the deacons of the craft guilds who were probably sympathetic to them, and dispersed. When the dragoons entered the city two hours later, they found it quiet. It was thought enough to arrest Finlay and one other leader, who were removed to Edinburgh. They were released after the Act of Union had been passed, or at least when the authorities believed the danger of insurrection to be over.

CHAPTER THREE

EIGHTEENTH-CENTURY FLOURISH

I n *Rob Roy* Scott has his Glasgow merchant Bailie Nicol Jarvie declare:

There's naething sae gude on this side o' time but it might hae been better, and that may be said o' the Union. Nane were keener against it than the Glasgow folk, wi' their rabblings and their risings, and their mobs, as they ca' them nowadays. But it's an ill wind blaws naebody gude – let ilka ane roose the ford as they find it – I say, Let Glasgow flourish! whilk is judiciously and elegantly putten round the town's arms by way of byword. Now since St Mungo catched herrings in the Clyde, what was ever like to gar us flourish like the sugar and tobacco trade? Will onybody tell me that, and grumble at the Treaty that opened us a road west-awa yonder.

The irony of the situation was not lost on the good Bailie, though Scott grants him a certain prescience; since the action of the novel takes place around the 1715 Jacobite Rising, less than ten years after the passing of the Treaty, the efflorescent effect of the sugar and tobacco trades was still in the future. Nevertheless the anachronism was justified, the Bailie's point being worth making. Whatever the defects of the Treaty, whatever cause for regret may be found in the achievement of Union – and Scott's own view was shifting and ambivalent – it was the creation of the free trade market within the British Isles, and the removal of restrictions which had prohibited trade between Scotland and the English colonies in the West Indies and America, that enabled Glasgow to flourish. The twin foundations of its prosperity were these sugar and tobacco trades, and when Glasgow came to boast itself 'the second city of the Empire', it paid unconscious tribute to the beneficence of the Union. Indeed the Union 'made' Glasgow, and the prosperity of Glasgow did much to justify the Union to generations of Scots.

At the time of the Union it was a small city of something between 12,000 and 15,000 inhabitants. Opinions vary and in the absence of an official census no figure can be reliable. Some consider that it had declined a little in population in the previous half-century, but this seems unlikely. Defoe found it:

> a large stately and well-built city, standing on a plain in a manner four-square, and the five principal streets are the fairest for breadth and the finest built I have ever seen in one city together. The houses are all of stone, and generally uniform in height as well as in front; the lower stories [of those near the Cross], for the most part, stand on vast square Doric columns with arches which open into the shops, adding to the strength as well as the beauty of the building. In a word 'tis one of the cleanliest, most beautiful and best built cities in Great Britain.

The impression of cleanliness was no doubt comparative, for the streets were unpaved and, despite the repeated objections of the magistrates, householders still deposited their middens in the public way. Moreover, only two street-cleaners were employed till 1777 (by which date the population had multiplied five times) when the Council resolved to take on a third man.

Other travellers agreed with Defoe. Edward Burt, an English officer on General Wade's staff, visited the city in 1726 and found 'a spacious carrefour where stands the cross, and going round it you have by turns the views of the four streets that in regular angles proceed from thence. The houses are faced with ashlar stone; they are well sashed, all of one model, and piazzas rise round them on either side, which gives a good air to the buildings. There are some handsome streets; but the extreme parts of the town are mean and disagreeable to the eye.' Despite this he found the town 'the most uniform and prettiest' he had ever seen.

Though the city would expand so rapidly, it remained possible to praise its beauty. A hundred years later the great journalist William Cobbett found its eighteenth-century development 'built in style, and beautiful in all ways, very little short of the New Town of Edinburgh... the whole of the city, compared to which the plastered-up Regent Street [London] is beggarly, is as fine as anything I ever saw, the New Town of Edinburgh excepted. The whole is built of beautiful white stone; and doors, windows, and everything bespeak solid worth, without any taste for ostentation or show.'

The Trongate was now the chief street for business, the Saltmarket that in which the principal merchants, like Bailie Nicol Jarvie himself, resided. The Trongate was then colonnaded, with small shops crammed into the galleries. The climate of Glasgow being damp, this covered market was desirable – the first umbrella was not seen in the city till 1783. Sixteen public wells provided the water-supply, though there were also a number of wells in several closes of the town. Living was still medieval in certain respects: only salt meat was normally available from Martinmas to May. Should any fresh meat be unexpectedly available in winter, the city's bellman paraded the streets to spread the news.

It was never an aristocratic city, though a few people of title might occupy tenement flats off a common stair, and though the so-called tobacco lords constituted a merchant élite unparallelled in eighteenth century Scotland, flat-dwelling was the norm, as in Edinburgh, Paris or Italian cities. There were almost no mansions or single houses, in the modern sense of the word, till the tobacco wealth began to change the city in the middle of the century.

Life was unpretentious. Doctor Alexander Carlyle, a famous Church of Scotland minister, recalling student days in Glasgow in the 1740s, wrote that 'there were only a few families of ancient citizens pretending to be gentlemen, and a few others who were recent settlers there who had obtained wealth and consideration in trade. The rest were shopkeepers and mechanics and successful pedlars, who occupied large ware-rooms full of manufactures of all sorts to furnish a cargo for Virginia. Their manner of life was coarse and vulgar.'

They were roused at six by the firing of a gun. This was the signal that the post had arrived from Edinburgh. Breakfast would consist of porridge, herring, bannocks and ale; tea was an expensive luxury till the middle of the century at least, a pound of green tea or the more expensive bohea costing more than eighteen bottles of claret and less than half the price of a leg of beef. The heavy duty on tea encouraged smuggling, and this brought down the price at which it might be available. Nevertheless, though Duncan Forbes of Culloden, Lord President of the Court of Session, was bewailing the popularity of tea by the 1740s and proposing that an Act of Parliament should be passed to prohibit 'under sufficient Penaltys... the use of Tea among that class of Mankind in this Country whose circumstances do not permit them to come at Tea that pays the duty', it seems by then to have made little headway in Glasgow. The herring were a different matter, however; Defoe considered that they cured the herring so excellently, that a Glasgow herring was as good as a Dutch one and superior to anything that could be found in England.

After breakfast business was pursued till the Tron Kirk bells rang at half past eleven and whoever could afford it retired to a tavern to take his meridian of ale or brandy. This was known as 'pewthering' since the drink was served in pewter tankards. Dinner, the main meal of the day, followed. In 1602 a King's Commission had decreed what this should consist of at the University of Glasgow. Masters should be served with white bread and ale;

a choice of soup; a piece of beef (fresh or salt) and of boiled mutton; two roasts, veal, mutton, chicken, rabbit or pigeon. The less fortunate undergraduates were to have oat bread, broth or pease pudding, and a dish of beef; they were to get a quart of ale between four of them. The domestic dinner, even a century later, would hardly offer such a choice as the university masters enjoyed; but the ingredients were similar, depending on wealth and status. After dinner business resumed till the early evening when the shops closed, men repaired again to the tavern before returning home for supper and bed around nine o'clock.

Drink played a substantial part in social and daily life. Professional men met their clients in taverns, deals were struck there. Clubs met there. Social life would have been inconceivable without them. Evidence of drunkenness is, however, contradictory, as might be expected. The English officer James Wolfe, the future conqueror of Quebec , told his mother in 1753 that at suppers 'the men drink till they are excessively drunk.' On the other hand, Thomas Reid, who became Professor of Moral Philosophy at Glasgow in 1763, found Glasgow a sober city: 'Though their religion is of a gloomy and enthusiastic sort, it makes them tame and sober. I have not heard either of a house or a head broken, of a pocket picked or any flagrant crime, since I came here. I have not heard any swearing in the streets, nor even seen a man drunk (excepting, *inter nos*, one professor) since I came.' Few of his successors could have said as much.

Trade, however, was Glasgow's business, and from soon after the Union a rapidly expanding one. Back in 1651 Cromwell had sent a Commissioner, named Tucker, north to report on the revenue of the Scottish Customs & Excise. He reported of Glasgow:

With the exception of the collegers, all the inhabitants are traders; some to Ireland with small smiddy coals, in open boats, from four to ten tons, from whence they bring hoops, rungs, barrel staves, meal, oats and butter; some to France, with plaidings, coals and herrings, from which the return is salt, pepper, raisins and prunes; some to Norway for timber. There have likewise been some who have ventured as far as Barbados, but the loss which they sustained by being obliged to come home late in the year, has made them discontinue going there any more. The mercantile genius of the people is strong, if they were not checked and kept under by the shallowness of their river, every day more and more increasing and filling up, so that no vessel of any burden can come up nearer the town than fourteen miles, where they must unload and send up their timber on rafts, and all other commodities by three or four tons of goods at a time, in small cobbles or boats, of three, four or five, and none above six tons a boat. There is in this place a collector, a cheque and four writers. There are twelve vessels belonging to the merchants of this port, viz, three of 150 tons each, one of 140 tons, two of 100, one of 50, three of 30, one of 15, and one of 12; none of which comes up to the town – total, 957 tons.

The Darien disaster had seen Glasgow's trade decline from even this pitiful level. In the first years of the Union Glasgow merchants had no ships of their own capable of crossing the Atlantic, and had to charter them from Whitehaven. Sending out supercargoes of miscellaneous goods and bringing back tobacco from Virginia and Maryland, they were soon able to build ships of their own. The first, registered to Glasgow owners, built at Greenock, crossed the Atlantic in 1718. The Glasgow merchants had got a start in the trade which they were soon to dominate. In time they had secured a contract to supply tobacco to the Farmers-General of France – that huge state within a state which contracted for all the indirect taxes levied in France, maintained a private army and held profitable monopolies. Their success aroused the envy of English merchants to such an extent that those of Bristol, London, Liverpool and Whitehaven complained to the Treasury. They declared that Glasgow was evading tax and so cheating the Government. The charges were dismissed by Treasury investigators, who found that they were 'groundless, and proceed from a spirit of envy, and not from a regard to the interest of trade, or to the King's revenue'. Despite this complaints continued, and Glasgow merchants were embroiled in expensive lawsuits before, in the mid-1730s, the trade could be considered fairly and fully established. From that time it flourished; resident agents were set up in the American tobacco states – the Carolinas as well as Virginia and Maryland – and the tobacco lords became Glasgow's, and Scotland's, first millionaires.

The great days of the trade were comparatively brief: between about 1750 and the outbreak of the American Revolution in 1775. In that period Glasgow took more than half the American tobacco crop. The city was essentially a mart or entrepôt. The Navigation Acts by which the English Parliament once jealously preserved colonial trade for English merchants and excluded Scots as well as all other foreigners now worked to Glasgow's advantage. Most of the tobacco sold on the continent of Europe passed through Glasgow. During the Seven Years' War (1756–63) one merchant, John Glassford, owned twenty-five ships and his turnover was reckoned at £500,000 a year

In the year before the American Revolution some 40,000 hogsheads of tobacco came into Glasgow, and 80 per cent of this was re-exported, the chief market being Holland, itself an entrepôt, the second France. Forty-two merchant houses were engaged in this trade. Though some were to be ruined when the trade collapsed as a result of the American Revolution, the list of names contains many subsequently famous in Glasgow's and Scotland's business history: Speirs, Baird, Finlay, Weir, McCall, Dunlop, Dennistoun, Gammell, Buchanan, Coats, Wylie, Ritchie, Hannah, Ballantine. Many of these are common West of Scotland names, and the tobacco lords no more than distant connections of later merchants and manufacturers who made them famous again. Nevertheless the list shows the indigenous nature of the tobacco ascendancy, and the forty-two firms its extent. Some are perpetuated, like Buchanan, in the names of Glasgow streets, as is Virginia itself. The Merchant City, now being renovated, with great warehouses turned into flats, had its origins in the tobacco and sugar trades.

The tobacco lords were regarded as parvenus by old-established merchants in the city, and seem to have taken little part in civic affairs; too busy making money. They repaid official indifference by putting on a show. There was then only one pavement in Glasgow; known as the Plainstones it covered the middle stretch of the street fronting the Trongate piazza. The tobacco lords annexed it as their social territory, and paraded there in business hours in scarlet coats, cocked hats and full-bottomed wigs, and with gold-headed canes in their hands. They were full of their own consequence and had to be approached with circumspection; any ordinary Glasgow citizen who encroached on their territory might receive a blow from a tobacco lord's ebony cane.

There was a dark side to their magnificence. Though many of the outgoing ships carried Scottish goods – James Glassford, for instance, had interests in leather, brewing and chemicals, and was the brother-in-law of a Lord Provost, Archibald Ingram, who owned print works and a factory where ribbons were made – others transported negro slaves to the plantations. Some tobacco lords had bought plantations themselves, or at least acquired an interest in some, and there was a cruel logic in their decision to control the whole cycle of the tobacco trade, from the transporting of the human material which worked the fields, to the crop itself.

Some diversified before the American Revolution. Dunlop of Garnkirk and Carmyle bought land with tobacco profits, and mined coal from his estate. He was later, in 1789–90, with Andrew Houston, another tobacco lord, one of the founders of the Glasgow Ship Bank, the first bank in the West of Scotland. The next year, Glassford was instrumental in establishing the Thistle Bank. They thus provided some of the capital and the financial instruments that would facilitate Glasgow's development in the last decades of the century from a commercial to a manufacturing and industrial city.

The tobacco trade did not revive after the American Revolution. Freed from the commercial restrictions imposed by the British Parliament the Americans now handled their own trade, and exported directly to the continent of Europe. Since Glasgow's trade had concentrated on the European rather than the British market, it suffered accordingly. However, Glasgow's merchants already displayed the resilience which has been a characteristic of the city. They turned first to the West Indian trade, in which a few houses had dealt since the 1730s. Sugar and rum were the principal imports; Glasgow was the biggest sugar importer in Britain by the end of the century. Imports were so great that the price dropped; the Scottish sweet tooth was in process of being developed. The duty on tea was lowered by William Pitt, and this encouraged Glasgow merchants to venture into trade with the East, though the first ship from Glasgow to Calcutta, the *Earl of Buckinghamshire* belonging to James Finlay & Co, did not sail till the year after Waterloo.

The rapid growth in commercial traffic took place despite the inadequacy of the city's river. The Clyde at Glasgow is by nature a shallow stream; only fifteen inches deep at low water, its channel obstructed by sandbanks. In the early eighteenth century goods could be brought no further than Greenock or Port Glasgow, which had been created, with the first dry dock in Scotland, on land bought by the Town Council from Sir Robert Maxwell of Newark in 1662. The Broomielaw, however, fourteen miles up river from the Port, was still covered with the broom its name suggests, and the channel between it and the Port could accommodate only flat-bottomed craft used to transport goods from ship to mart. A quay, however, had been constructed at the Broomielaw in the last decade of the seventeenth century. Everyone was conscious of the need for improvement, doubtful how this could be effected. In 1740 the Council agreed 'that a tryal be made this season of deepning the river by carrying away the banks below the Broomielaw, and remitt to the magistrates to cause do the same, and go the length of £100 sterling of charges thereupon, and to cause built a flatt-bottomed boat for carying off the sand and chingle from the banks'. This seems to have met with little success, and in 1755 they commissioned a new survey. The engineer who undertook it reported that at low water the ford about two miles below Glasgow was 1ft 3in. deep; rising to 3ft 8in. at high tide. He recommended the construction of a weir and lock four miles below the city, to create a harbour 4ft 6in. deep. An Act of Parliament to allow this improvement was obtained, but not acted upon.

Uncertainty prevailed. Another survey was commissioned ten years later from the Cheshire engineer Golborne, who had experience in canal work. He reported that the river was still in a state of nature, and recommended that the channel should be narrowed for several miles below the city. This would – obviously – confine the water, make it act more effectively on the bottom, and make the channel deeper in proportion as it was narrower. A new Act of Parliament was obtained in 1770, a contract with Golborne signed in 1772, and three years later he had constructed 117 jetties, on both sides of the river, and improved it to such an extent that there was now more than 6ft of water at the Broomielaw at high tide. This was indeed more than he had promised, and the Town Council rewarded him for having improved on his contract by making a grant of £1500. They showed further gratitude by awarding him a silver cup, and making his son a present of £100. What the son had done to deserve this I don't know. The measure of Golborne's success, which was only the prelude to the considerable improvements which would take place in the next century may be measured by the increase in revenue, which rose from £1044 in 1771 to £3319 in 1800. That figure was to be dwarfed in the next half-century.

Contemporaries recognised that Glasgow was a city given over to business. In his *History of the Scottish People 1580–1830*, T. C. Smout provides comparative tables of occupations in Glasgow and Edinburgh in the second half of the eighteenth century. Drawing on street directories and examining a thousand entries taken at random, he demonstrates the markedly different social composition of the two cities. Edinburgh has more than five times as many who describe themselves as nobles and gentry, and more than twice as many professional men. On the other hand Glasgow has two and a half times more merchants and manufacturers, and 40 per cent more in the category of 'small tradesmen, artisans, craftsmen, "mechanics" etc'. Categorisation is difficult since some of those who described themselves as gentry were probably merchants who also possessed estates. He observes that: 'the expression "manufacturer", which occurs repeatedly in the Glasgow directory, is not known at all in the Edinburgh one. It is interesting that in Edinburgh nearly one in three of all the entrants in the directory was a professional man, and one in eight a "businessman": in Glasgow one in eight was a professional man, and one in three a businessman – exactly the reverse proportions if the source is an accurate guide.'

By the end of the eighteenth century Glasgow was poised for a boom. The population had risen to over 80,000. The figure at the first official census in 1801 was 83,769. From that figure it would rise at extraordinary speed. The city was spreading in all directions, swallowing up villages such as Anderston, Bridgeton and Calton, all of which had been laid out by early industrialists, filling the open country between them and the old city. The energy that inspired this expansion was stupendous; it was also intelligent.

The eighteenth century has been called the Golden Age of Scottish culture. With justice: Scotland was pre-eminent in philosophy, economics, natural and applied science. The University of Glasgow played a full part in this. At the beginning of the century it was, like the other Scottish Universities at St Andrews, Aberdeen and Edinburgh, little more than a grammar school, where lectures were delivered in Latin to uncomprehending students; its function was to train men for the ministry, and its professors and regents were more concerned to regulate their charges' behaviour and supervise their moral development than to train them to think, or educate them in the full sense of the word. By 1750 all this had changed. If the University of Glasgow was not quite as famous as Edinburgh – then, in the opinion of many, the finest university in Europe – it ran it a close second. It was famous in all branches of learning.

Nobody contributed more to this development than Francis Hutcheson, who held the Chair of Moral Philosophy from 1729 till 1746. Hutcheson was an Ulsterman who, like many of his fellow countrymen, had taken his degree in Glasgow. He was a philosopher of distinction who can lay claim to being the father of Scottish philosophy. His development of the moral-sense theory which postulated that men had a natural inclination to virtue, and compared the moral with the aesthetic sense, both being natural attributes of man, was a powerful influence on David Hume. Yet Hutcheson's influence on Glasgow, and on university teaching in general, was much simpler, and even more profound. He began lecturing in English. The aid to understanding, and therefore to intellectual enthusiasm, was considerable; with the first sentence which he uttered in a tongue his students could understand, Hutcheson removed the University from the medieval to the modern world.

His understanding of what was meant by philosophy was wide and comprehensive. He took moral philosophy to include jurisprudence as well as ethics; his lectures considered the principles of law and government, which involved him in a discussion of economics. This was the basis of the Scottish Science of Man which joined metaphysics to morality and ethics to economics.

Adam Smith succeeded Hutcheson as Professor of Moral Philosophy in 1751, and remained in Glasgow for eleven years; they were, by his own account, the happiest of his life. It was there that he wrote his first book, *The Theory of Moral Sentiments* (1759), which would lead him by a process of logical intellectual development to his most important work, *The Wealth of Nations* (1776). Smith's moral and economic philosophy was singularly attuned to the society he saw developing around him in Glasgow. According to him, man's habit of sympathetic association, his capacity for personal affection, and for the pursuit of a rational, and therefore self-limiting, self-interest, would promote economic development, unless hindered by the restrictive regulatory activity of government. Now, eighteenth-century Scotland was a society unusually free of government; in Sir Walter Scott's words, Scotland was left 'under the guardianship of her own institutions, to win her silent way to national wealth and consequence'. But Smith could also observe that Glasgow was ready to accept men of ability, whatever their background, into the business community. The restrictions imposed by the medieval guilds had largely disappeared before Smith came to Glasgow; he could remark the consequence. Whereas his reading and travels had let him see how the protective ethos of the guilds restrained economic development, his experience of Glasgow reinforced the theory he was forming that free trade and man's natural 'propensity to truck, barter and exchange' could work towards a general prosperity in an expanding economy. No doubt, Smith would have come to the conclusion if he had never lived in Glasgow; nevertheless he was impressed by the evidence the city offered.

The University itself was expanding. At the beginning of the century it had only a little over 400 students; by 1800 this had more than doubled. The University authorities encouraged them to live within the college, where they could be adequately supervised. This was the more necessary as it was still customary to proceed to university at the age of fourteen or fifteen. The University year lasted from October to May. Many of the students were poor, and there was an ancient privilege in Glasgow that oatmeal intended for their use should be exempt from the town customs exacted from all provisions sold in the market. When this rule was broken on one occasion, the University deputed Smith to appeal to the Town Council; which he did all the more willingly because he considered the imposition of such internal tolls or customs duties to be a hindrance to economic development.

Whereas Edinburgh increasingly drew undergraduates from England, especially from the Nonconformists who were debarred by religious tests from entering Oxford and Cambridge, Glasgow attracted undergraduates from Ireland. These were mostly from the Presbyterian community of Ulster, themselves the descendants of Scottish settlers. Adam Smith's successor, as Professor of Moral Philosophy, Thomas Reid, remarked that 'near a third of our students are Irish. Thirty came over lately in one vessel. We have a good many English and some foreigners. Many of the Irish as well as Scotch are poor, and come up late to save money.'

At the beginning of the century most undergraduates were still preparing for the ministry; by its end a university education had become more generally valued. The range of subjects studied had widened, and, though Scottish universities never abandoned the idea of vocational education, the conception of the university's function had also broadened. The Universities of Glasgow and Edinburgh became famous for their teaching of science – Smout calls the medical men of the two cities 'a Pleiades of talent'; the great chemists William Cullen and Joseph Black both held in succession Chairs at Glasgow and Edinburgh. Yet there was nothing narrow in their understanding of scientific discipline: George Davie in *The Democratic Intellect* (1961) has characterised eighteenth-century Scottish science as having a metaphysical and humanistic bias. Disdaining educational specialisation, scientists such as Cullen and Black were as concerned as philosophers like Hutcheson, Hume and Smith to place their subject within a general or comprehensive culture. The object of scientific study was not merely the mastery of certain techniques or of a topic abstracted from any general context in order to be examined in isolation; it was, rather, an intellectual pursuit with social implications which were discussed as an essential part of the exercise. Science was conceived as being neither rarefied as in the concept of pure science, nor merely technical or utilitarian. Research was conducted for its own sake, in order to confirm first principles; there was an intense concern for the foundations of knowledge. At the same time it was accepted that the advancement of knowledge and understanding would lead to practical improvements. So Joseph Black, for instance, investigated matters of practical concern to the agricultural improvers: soil analysis and the effect of fertilisers.

A more famous example of the interplay between science and technology is offered by the career of James Watt. Watt, born in Greenock in 1736, was employed by the University to repair and, if need be, improvise instruments used in the Department of Mathematics. In this capacity he attracted the attention of Professor Black, who befriended and advised him, then financed his early experiments. Black had himself made the discovery of latent heat and its corollary, the theory of specific heat; this helped Watt to formulate the idea of a separate condenser, which proved the means of developing Newcomen's steam-pump and so creating the power which made the Industrial Revolution possible. It is scarcely an exaggeration to claim that the nineteenth century, the Age of Steam, began in the laboratory of the University of Glasgow. Watt moved away from Glasgow to develop his engines commercially in Birmingham in partnership with Matthew Boulton; before he did so, he had also been involved in survey work on the Forth & Clyde Canal, and in the deepening of the Clyde.

Cullen and Black both aimed to make science 'a study for every man of good education'. Their influence on the development of Glasgow is incalculable. Both encouraged people from outside the University to attend their lectures, and the advances in industrial chemistry were certainly made by men who were influenced by them. It is true that significant developments in textile chemistry – turkey-red dyeing and the invention of a bleaching powder which formed the basis of the fortune of the Tennant family – came from abroad; but the habit of mind which encouraged a ready and constant responsiveness to innovation was formed in the Scottish universities. Smout puts it exactly: 'One of a university teacher's main functions is to inspire people with curiosity: if eighteenth-century Scotland had curiosity in such good measure it was surely due in no small degree to men like Joseph Black.'

One offshoot of this curiosity came into being at the end of the century. This was Anderson's Institution, established by the will of John Anderson, himself Professor of Moral Philosophy in the University. Situated in George Street, its purpose was the wider diffusion of education, particularly among those who, for one reason or another, were incapable of following a university course. (One reason for this might be gender: women were not admitted to the University, but they were welcome to attend lectures at the Institution.) Its first teacher was Anderson's successor in his University Chair, Thomas Garnett, who described the Institution as being 'undoubtedly well adapted to the education of young gentlemen designed for commerce or manufacture who are too often sent from the grammar school to the counting house without acquiring that knowledge which will enable them to fill up in a rational manner the vacant hours... or which will enable him to make those improvements in his business he would do if acquainted with the principles on which his different operations depend.'

The philosophy of the Institution was therefore characteristic of late eighteenth-century Scotland; it would join an examination of first principles to the acquisition of knowledge that would be of practical utility. The Institution was intended to bring a literary and scientific education within the reach of everyone who wished to acquire one. It was democratic and optimistic, an expression of faith in the human capacity for improvement, made and coming into being at a time when the Establishment's fears of the seditious contagion of the principles of the French Revolution were breeding reaction and repression. This mood bypassed Glasgow. The Institution offered 'a complete scientific course on physics and chemistry with their application to the arts and manufactures', and other courses on botany, mathematics, agriculture and modern languages. These courses were attended annually by between 500 and 1000 students, at a time when the population of the city was less than 100,000. No doubt some of the students, particularly some of the young ladies, were less than wholly serious; but the faith displayed by the Institution's founders and its governing body in the value of widely diffused education reflected Glasgow's development into an Open Society where a man would be judged more by his contribution to social welfare and prosperity than by his birth or status. Modern Glasgow has always been a self-consciously democratic city, one which has retained vertical attachments throughout society, and been suspicious of horizontal stratification. It owes something of this character to the same influences and convictions which brought Anderson's Institution into being, and sustained it, till it eventually became the University of Strathclyde. Doctor Garnett's successor was George Birkbeck, who took the Andersonian principle further by being responsible, in 1823, for the establishment of the Mechanics' Institute 'for the purpose of diffusing knowledge on literary and scientific subjects among the operatives of Glasgow'. Birkbeck had, in fact, by that time moved to London where he established a similar institution in 1824 (now part of the University of London), but the confidence that the wider dissemination of education was of social, as well as personal, utility, may be traced to his experience of Glasgow. So successful was the Mechanics' Institute in Glasgow that, within twenty-five years of its foundation, it had more than 600 students, variously listed as clerks, warehousemen, mechanics, millwrights, engineers, joiners, cabinet-makers, iron-founders, masons, shoemakers, tailors, smiths and weavers. It was on such men, eager for self-improvement, that Glasgow would draw in the years of incomparably rapid expansion that were to follow. Whatever the horrors that resulted from the pace and conditions of industrialisation, the city that would make itself in the succeeding hundred years was a consequence of the Scottish Enlightenment, the expression of the Enlightenment's faith in man's ability to form his world according to his will and the operation of his intelligence. For this reason, though architecturally Glasgow was to be made as a Victorian city, its essence is to be found in the previous century.

The Enlightenment is customarily associated with Edinburgh, with sufficient reason. But if we are to seek its consequence we will find it rather in the dynamism of nineteenth-century Glasgow than in the conservatism of Edinburgh then. For those whose view is restricted to the nation's capital, it can seem that by 1832 the Enlightenment had fizzled out. Glasgow tells a different story. It shows Enlightenment principles and faith still in working order. It shows a new world being made.

CHAPTER FOUR

NINETEENTH CENTURY: HEYDAY AND HELL

There are two histories of nineteenth-century Glasgow. They are distinct and contradictory. The two cities they describe might seem to belong to different times, different worlds, even to inhabit different moral universes. Yet they lay one on top of the other, and the problem for the historian, who would seek to reconcile these differences in a single narrative, is that both histories are true, both cities really existed, success was as real and satisfying as failure was horrible. And the matter is more complicated still, for these apparently distinct histories of different cities are in reality the story of the same city as seen from different angles; and the cities were not in reality distinct, for not only did one lie on the other, each penetrated the other, each depended on the other, and countless men and women moved through both, inhabiting both either at different periods of their lives, or, even more conspicuously, living in both simultaneously.

The history of Victorian Glasgow is one of triumph, of an expanding economy, a city growing ever richer and more splendid, erecting magnificent public and domestic buildings, a city rich in high culture, notable for piety and philanthropy, for the provision of comfort, luxuries and security on a scale which would have amazed even the richest of its citizens a hundred years earlier.

But it is also a story of degradation and misery, of the fierce exploitation of man by man. A Reporter of the West of Scotland Handloom Weavers Commission said:

> I have seen human degradation in some of its worst phases, both in England and abroad, but I can advisedly say that I did not believe until I visited the wynds of Glasgow that so large an amount of filth, crime, misery and disease existed in one spot in any civilised country.

Doctor Neil Arnot, who collaborated with Edwin Chadwick in his Reports on the *Sanitary Conditions of the Labouring Classes in Scotland* (1842), penetrated these wynds. He found that:

The interiors of these houses and their inmates corresponded with the exteriors. We saw half-dressed wretches crowding together to be warm; and in one bed, although in the middle of the day, several women were imprisoned under a blanket, because as many others who had on their backs all the articles of dress that belonged to the party were then out of doors in the streets. The picture is so shocking that, without ocular proof, one would be disposed to doubt the possibility of the facts.

But the facts were there, and remained there. As late as 1886 one-third of Glasgow's families lived in single-room flats. Thirty years later the Royal Commission on Housing found that 'there were more than four persons per room in 10.9 per cent of Glasgow's houses, over three persons in 27.9 per cent and over two in 55.7 per cent'. In 1902 the city's Medical Officer of Health Dr Chalmers noted that 30 per cent of infantile deaths occurred among the 14 per cent of the population accommodated in single-room houses. One of his predecessors, Dr Russell, gave an unforgettable picture of what that might involve:

> their little bodies are laid on a table or on a dresser so as to be somewhat out of the way of their brothers and sisters, who play and sleep and eat in their ghastly company. From beginning to rapid-ending the lives of these children are short. One in every five of all who are born there never see the end of their first year.

Disease was rife in this second city. During the cholera and typhus epidemics of the 1840s the death-rate in Glasgow rose to 40 per 1000 inhabitants. The tenement flats were infested with bugs and cockroaches, the drinking-water was unsafe, indeed positively harmful, till in 1859 fresh water was brought from Loch Katrine by thirteen miles of tunnelling and 'twenty-five important iron and masonry aqueducts over rivers and ravines'.

The poor lived then in stinking and ill-ventilated tenements, piled up on top of each other, breeding-houses of infection. The inhabitants' easiest solace was alcohol; it was often their only one. Crime, brutality and violence were commonplace. It was hard to imagine that there could be a worse place out of hell.

Yet this was also the city offering horizons of endless possibility, of self-improvement and educational zeal, a city of enormous luxury in which the *Glasgow Herald* could, in 1855, describe 'Messrs Wylie & Lochhead's new establishment, 45 Buchanan Street,' as surpassing 'as a place of business anything of which we have seen or heard'. The newspaper commended and wondered at the new device, 'a very ingenious hoisting apparatus':

Parties who are old, fat, feeble, short-winded, or simply lazy, or who desire a bit of fun, have only to place themselves on an enclosed platform or flooring, when they are elevated by a gentle and pleasing process, to a height exceeding that of a country steeple, and from the railing of the upper gallery, they may look down on a scene of industrial activity and artistic magnificence which as yet has not a parallel amongst us...

This contrast between the two cities has to be remembered, or understood to exist below the surface of everything which is written about Glasgow in its period of growth and apparent decline. Admittedly, the contrast is not unique to Glasgow; similar discrepancies could be observed in London, Liverpool, Manchester, Leeds or the industrial cities of northern Europe and the United States. For the fact is that the story of every city from around 1800 is a tale of two cities. It is not simply a matter of wealth, though it is also, of course, always a matter of wealth. There have always been distinctions of wealth in cities, but, from about that date, the scale expanded and the conditions of life within the cities changed out of all recognition, as indeed did the relation of these cities to the country around them. What happened was first a loss of homogeneity. In one sense this meant simply that the city ceased to be a comprehensible thing, a describable entity. When we read Defoe's account of Glasgow at the time of the Union, we can believe that he is giving us the essence of its totality. We can believe that it is possible for him to understand the whole city, and, from reading him and historians who write about eighteenth-century Glasgow, we can trust that we have some considerable degree of knowledge of how everybody in the city lived, and of what their relations with each other were. Glasgow at the time of the Union was still small enough, and coherent enough, and personal enough, to be considered as an entity. A hundred years later this was no longer true, and it became less true as the nineteenth century passed. It will never be true again.

The instrument of this change was Industrialism and the Industrial System – the distinctive form of capitalist production and exchange marked by the division of labour, and the division of the rewards of labour. Industrialism is not, and probably can never be, a neutral term. Though it may be employed with the intention simply of describing a certain historical process, it is impossible to disengage it from value-judgement. Its energising force was competition, which the medieval guild system that it finally replaced had tried to outlaw. For those most conscious of the benefits brought by Industrialism, competition is itself a natural and fructifying force; for those whose gaze is turned towards the second city of squalor, misery and degradation, competition is no more than the expression of greed, working itself out in disregard for human suffering or for the wider and more far-reaching effects of economic activity. Critics of Industrialism see it as brute force, paying no heed to human life, throwing individual lives aside as its high priests bow down to Moloch. It deprived men of property and natural rights, and reduced them to the status of tools, no more valuable – as being less durable and representing a lower level of capital investment – than the machines they worked. The Papal Encyclical of 1891, *Rerum Novarum*, issued by Leo XIII, though written by Cardinal Manning, attacked 'the callousness of employers and the greed of unrestrained competition'; it declared that 'a small number of very rich men' had become able 'to lay upon the masses of the poor a yoke little better than slavery'. The theory of Socialism would arise in opposition to the capitalist theory of Industrialism; but I quote for preference the Papal Encyclical, because it represents an older strain. It speaks for the view of the social order from which Industrialism emerged as a rebellious child.

And for its admirers the rebellious child was defensible. Industrialism greatly increased the total wealth of the world and raised the general standard of living of those countries which experienced it. Its logical end was a condition of greatly increased wealth, and much greater leisure, for a growing number.

Nor is that all. The market economy, diminishing the power of the authoritarian State, widening the choice available to citizens as consumers, has been a means of spreading freedom. Wherever it has taken root, political freedom has eventually followed, and even found its full expression in the greatest of freedoms, which is freedom from politics.

Yet this wealth, leisure and freedom have been built on the reduction of millions of men and women to dismal poverty, intense, painful and soul destroying labour, and to a state of servitude, though one lacking the legal protection at times accorded to slaves.

Glasgow in the first half of the nineteenth century displays the Industrial System developing in pure, unchecked form. Its subsequent history may be read as an attempt to correct its abuses, without destroying its vitality or losing its benefits. In a third stage, as the market forces which had favoured Glasgow turned against the city, can be seen attempts made to check their operation; and finally, in the most modern period, Glasgow can be observed moving, though now in hesitant and uncertain fashion, towards a new sense of its own capabilities and the assumption of new functions. What may also be seen is that the period of apparent decline, when Glasgow lost its self confidence and its primacy in the industrial world, was also a period when the blessings of Industrialism were being more widely shared, even as the city itself appeared to be moving steadily into a post-industrial age.

The city's expansion was incomparably rapid. The population rose from 83,769 in 1801 to 147,043 in 1821 and 282,134 in 1841. It trebled over the next seventy years, to 784,000 in 1911. This figure, however, excluded burghs such as Govan and Partick still administratively separate from Glasgow though in human terms within the city's boundaries. Had they been included, the population would have been over the million mark.

It was, however, the population growth of the first half of the nineteenth century which fixed the pattern, and which was also something altogether new. These incomers constituted a proletariat with no tradition of urban living, drawn to the city by the mechanics of the industrial system which required hands to work its machines. They had to be housed, and they were housed as quickly and cheaply as possible. First, the old parts of the city were abandoned to them as the middle classes who had benefited from the expansion of commerce, and were now benefiting directly or indirectly from the new industries, moved to the new districts being built over to the west. The University, with its spacious court and gardens, was soon surrounded by dense and vile slums. The city's mid-nineteenth-century historian, James Pagan, writing just before the University moved to Gilmorehill, wrote:

> When it is considered that the old college lies in the heart of a great manufacturing population – that north and south it is only separated by narrow and dirty lands or vennels, from the dwelling places of dense masses of the lowest of the population, among whom filth and fever never cease to be – it is not surprising that the professors should be anxious to transfer their academic halls and dwelling-houses from this polluted locality...

One of those in favour of the move was the great physicist Lord Kelvin; his brother had died from typhus, which Kelvin believed had come over the wall from one of two streets, the Havannah and the New Vennel, which were reckoned the dirtiest in the whole city.

The new Glaswegians swarmed into the city from the immediate countryside; as the Highland glens were cleared of people to make way for sheep in the 1820s, the city was colonised by Gaelic-speaking Highlanders; then, when blight struck the Irish potato crop in the 1840s, by desperate immigrants. It is a measure of the city's expanding economy that there were jobs for them.

They were to be found in cotton mills, bleaching works, dyeworks, iron foundries, commerce, and, increasingly in shipbuilding and steelworks. Shipbuilding was to be the Glasgow industry *par excellence*, but it was preceded by others, notably textiles, on which the city's first industrial, as distinct from commercial, wealth was based. Textiles spawned ancillary industries, notably chemicals. The history of the Tennant family offers an instructive example of Glasgow capitalism at work in this sector.

The Tennants were originally bonnet lairds in Ayrshire. The founder of their fortune was Charles Tennant (1768–1838). His father, John Tennant of Glenconner, was a friend of Burns who celebrated him in verse as 'gude auld Glen/The ace an' wale of honest men'. Charles Tennant, known as 'Wabster Charlie', started a bleachfield in Paisley, producing a solution of chloride of lime which was an effective bleaching agent. Then he moved to Glasgow founding the St Rollox Works within a quarter of a mile of the Cathedral. By 1825 this had become the largest chemical works in the world. It was based on a French process known, after its inventor, as the Leblanc process, which involved the decomposition of salt by sulphuric acid; its significance was that it freed the industry from reliance on natural or organic sources such as kelp. It was not agreeable, for it polluted the atmosphere of the locality with sulphurous fumes and deposits of alkali waste. Nor did the standing tanks of urine (the cheapest source of ammonia) improve the amenities. Commercially, however, it was of enormous benefit, and not only to the Tennants.

The St Rollox Works made available a bleach that reduced the cost of whitening cloth while standardising the process. The chemical works had the same influence on the glass, textiles, paper, and soap industries. By 1818 the Tennants were manufacturing soda crystals and soap themselves. Charles's son John (1796–1878) entered the business as a chemist in 1815. In 1838 he became general manager and head of the firm which he continued to guide till his death. An attempt was made to tackle the problem of pollution by building a 435-ft chimney; known as Tennant's Stalk this dominated the Glasgow skyline, and at least diffused the atmospheric pollution over a wider area. Other problems of pollution, inseparable from the Leblanc process – vast accumulations of solid waste and a yellow sulphurous discharge which contaminated local streams – were not tackled for another thirty years. One paradox of Industrialism was revealed: it created wealth and it contributed to a general raising of living standards – in the case of the Tennants the production of cheap soap probably improved general standards of hygiene. At the same time the by-products of the industrial process were noxious.

The Tennant interests were not restricted to the St Rollox Works. This becomes more obvious when one looks at the career of John's more famous son, Charles, but John Tennant was himself active in what would now be called diversification. He took a share in the establishment of the Tharsis Sulphur & Copper Company, of which more later. Tennants operated a drysaltery from an office in Cochrane Street, and dealt also in madders (a plant which yields a red dye), olive oil and wine. John Tennant also invested in the mid-century railway boom.

Though John Tennant had overseas interests (in the Buffalo & Lake Huron Railway, Californian gold-mines, and cocoa and sugar estates in Trinidad, for instance), and though in 1864 Tennants had established other chemical works on Tyneside, John remained essentially a Glasgow business-man. He was active in local politics, having been prominent in the group of Glasgow Whigs who supported the Reform Bill of 1832, and in the agitation for the repeal of the Corn Laws. He was, naturally, a Free Trader; one consequence of the repeal of the Corn Laws was that, by lowering the price of bread, it enabled manufacturers to keep wages down.

His son Charles was a more notable figure. He had an audacity his father lacked, and starting from a secure position as a third-generation industrial-ist, he broke the bounds within which John had been happy to remain confined. While Charles did much to forge links between the City of London and manufacturing interests in Glasgow and the North of England, he was also one of the first, great Glasgow industrialists to remove himself from his home base, set up as a country gentleman and enter, as if by right, metropolitan society. John Tennant was a powerful man in Glasgow and the West of Scotland; his son, made a baronet by Gladstone in 1886, was a truly imperial figure. In a sense he symbolises Glasgow's own development from being a provincial city to one holding its vaunted status of the second city of the Empire.

Sir Charles Tennant's success was equal to his daring. Branching out on his own as a young man, he set up the trading company of Tennant, Knox & Co, based in London, which acted as an agent for Charles Tennant & Son. A venture in an Australian Land Company, when he was only twenty-five, made him a profit of £80,000 and enabled him to purchase the estate of Glen in Peeblesshire. His greatest coup, however, was the purchase of the pyrites mines of Tharsis in southern Spain. This was logical, since pyrites, being some 48 per cent sulphur, was a valuable component of alkali. But this purchase also gave him an interest in the other elements of pyrites, copper, iron, gold and silver. By 1872 he had bought seven metal-extraction companies to work the ore, one of them established near the St Rollox Works. Involvement in the technology of metallurgy led to the purchase of Indian gold-mines. The Cassel Gold Extraction Company was formed. Initially it was a failure, but three Tennant employees, working in a tenement flat at 319 Crown Street, Glasgow, developed a process by which the gold recoverable from pyrites was raised from just over 50 per cent to 95 per cent. Tennant's company bought the patent from their employees. It revolutionised gold-mining, and the Tennant subsidiary, Cassel, charged a royalty for its use under licence.

He now turned to iron. In an attempt to use the 'blue billy ore' he had accumulated from his pyrites workings, he formed, in association with others in the chemical and metallurgy businesses, the Steel Company of Scotland. Its plant was at Hallside in Glasgow, and mass production of steel in Scotland dates from its foundation in 1872. It was to dominate steel production in Scotland for twenty years. He formed another company, Nobel's Explosives Ltd, also with headquarters in Glasgow, to exploit Nobel's patents.

The first sixty years of Sir Charles Tennant's life saw almost unbroken success. He was the greatest figure in the Glasgow business world, and an enormous influence there. He was a director of the North British Railway and Chairman of the Union Bank of Scotland. Naturally, he became the centre of a group of succesful men with disposable capital who were eager to invest in his overseas ventures, and in so doing to extend Glasgow's interests abroad. In the last twenty years of his long life his empire came under stress, partly as a result of a national depression, partly as a result of misjudgements he had made, such as the decision not to participate in a joint venture in Germany which would have given his companies access to the energetic, science-based industry of the Rhineland, partly as a result of increasing competition in other fields from younger and perhaps sharper competitors, such as Colville's and the Consett works on Tyneside, rivals in steel-making.

Nevertheless Sir Charles Tennant spans the greatest period in Glasgow's industrial history. A statue sits serenely outside the Tennant family tomb in Glasgow's Necropolis, gazing in the direction of the St Rollox Works. The failures, or weaknesses visible in his empire, towards the end of his life do, however, indicate a certain fragility in his achievement, and in Glasgow's. The circumstances of the discovery of the Cassel Company's cyanide process are symptomatic; the laboratories which German and American companies were already establishing in order to carry out research and development contrast with the tenement flat in Crown Street where John MacArthur and the brothers Forrest hit on the process. Though the Edwardian years were to seem the apogee of Glasgow's prosperity, indications of subsequent decline were already apparent, or may be recognised in retrospect. Another symptom may be found in Tennant's changing politics. In old age he abandoned the Liberal belief in Free Trade, with which the family had been associated, and allied himself to Joseph Chamberlain who was calling for protective tariffs. Confidence in Britain's, and Glasgow's, ability to beat the rest of the world was already ebbing away.

With Sir Charles's death in 1906 the Tennant connection with Glasgow weakened. Throughout the nineteenth century they had been principal agents of wealth creation. Little of this had gone to the employees of the St Rollox Works, however. They were mostly Irish immigrants, and unskilled; the nascent trade union movement could do little with them, or for them. The health of many was ruined by the chemical processes with which they worked. They were ill paid. In 1879 the Tennant Works paid their 3000 employees an average of only £40 a year; Sir Charles Tennant left an estate in Britain worth more than £3 million.

An even more vivid example of the costs and rewards of Industrialism is afforded by another great Glasgow chemical firm, John & James White. This firm was founded in 1810 by John White who manufactured soap and soda at Shawfield on the Rutherglen Road. In 1830 it began to manufacture bichromate of potash or chrome, which became, on account of its success, almost its sole product. It was produced from chrome iron ore, imported from Turkey and Russia, and sold to textile manufacturers as a mordant, or agent, for fixing certain dyes, notably turkey red, logwood and chrome yellow. It later became an important agent in other manufacturing processes. It enjoyed an expanding market throughout the century, and the Whites went on adding to their works until they covered some twenty acres. They employed about 500 men and since their output was rather more than the sum total of that of their competitors, they held a dominant share of the market.

The employees, like those of Tennant's, were mostly Irish immigrants. Wages were low and they worked a twelve-hour day. According to Sydney Checkland in the *Dictionary of Scottish Business Biography*:

> It was their job to do the lifting, carrying, grinding, mixing, stirring, firing the many furnaces, removing the residues, working for the most time amid great heat and noxious fumes. There were the chrome furnacemen, the pearl ashmen, the crystal house men, the workers at the vitriol tanks, and the acid towers, together with the general labourers. The chemicals industry, indeed, in spite of being science based, produced the nadir of working conditions, a scene of terrible male degradation.

The factory inspectors, who had come into being as a result of Lord Althorp's Factory Act, as far back as 1833, found it particularly difficult to police chemical works, and it was not till 1902 that a doctor could tell the British Medical Association that it was years since he had seen 'the subject of mercurial tremors totally unable to lift the cup of cold water to his raw and burning lips'.

The degradation was not confined to those who worked in the industry, though they suffered worst; so badly indeed that employees at White's were known either as 'White's canaries', on account of the yellow dust which covered their clothes, or as 'White's dead men' owing to their faces being blanched by exposure to chemicals. But the whole area around the Shawfield Works was polluted. What had been common land and a playground for local children was covered with waste dumps, while a greenish-yellow liquid poured into the Clyde, still, until 1859, a source of drinking water.

Meanwhile the While family flourished, and did good works. The second generation, called like the founders John and James, bought themselves country estates on the shores of Loch Long, and built mansions in the best Scottish baronial style. They were all devoted and enthusiastic Free Churchmen, Liberals and philanthropists. The chief member of the third generation, John Campbell White, born in 1843, the year of the Disruption of the Kirk, was brought up in an atmosphere of intense piety. In his middle thirties he would be the West of Scotland's principal organiser for the American evangelists Moody and Sankey. He supported the Bible Society, the Christian Institute in Bothwell Street, and the Livingstonia Mission in Africa. He was the very model of a God-fearing Bible-reading Calvinist. The *Missionary Record* of the Free Kirk noted approvingly that 'in his office, his home, in a railway carriage, at the roadside he was ever ready to join one in prayer'. As befitted such a man, he maintained the family tradition of Liberalism; Gladstone made him a peer in 1893 officially for his philanthropic activities, also perhaps because of his generosity to the Liberal Party. White took the title of Lord Overtoun, the name he gave to a public park which he provided for the people of Rutherglen. He was a teetotaller, and a graduate of the University of Glasgow who had won prizes in Logic and Natural Philosophy. He was the prototype of the righteous businessman, who had made Glasgow great.

In 1899 an unprecedented strike broke out at Shawfield. Though the workers' demands were moderate, they were not satisfied, so the men turned to the Socialist leader, Keir Hardie, who was then editing the *Labour Leader*. He took up their cause and denounced Overtoun as a 'Holy Willie'. The dispute aroused all Glasgow, the more so when other newspapers looked into the matter, and people realised that Hardie's attack was not just an example of left-wing agitation. The revelation that the men were paid less than five shillings for a twelve-hour day, that they worked in appalling conditions which led to respiratory and digestive diseases, was contrasted with Lord Overtoun's comfortable life in his mansion, one wall of which was covered with illuminated addresses paid him by grateful recipients of his charity. All he could say in reply was that his Shawfield Works had satisfied the factory inspectorate and that the wages he paid were no lower than the going rate for unskilled work. It was not very convincing, but with the offer of a few concessions – minor improvements in working conditions and a modest rise in wages – he was able to persuade the strikers to return to work. He died nine years later, leaving estate valued at almost £700,000 and the obituaries were generally admiring.

It is easy to condemn men such as the Tennants and Whites as exploiters, careless or contemptuous of the lives deformed or ruined in their service. Their greed, and that of hundreds like them, appears naked; Overtoun's hypocrisy monstrous. The contrast between Sir Charles Tennant admiring his Gainsboroughs or Turners in the library of his London house in Grosvenor Square, or Lord Overtoun intoning passages of the Bible to admiring congregations, while the Irish labourers who toiled in their works coughed and spewed their way to an early grave, is too sharp to be comfortably entertained. Yet without such men the wealth which gave Glasgow magnificent public buildings and which fostered a large and cultivated middle class, would not have existed; even the wretched Irish would have failed to find any employment, and have suffered accordingly.

The poet Edwin Muir, whose reflections on Glasgow will be considered more fully in a later chapter, observed in the 1930s: 'if Industrialism were suddenly to stop now, and we had to judge it by its past history, it would appear like a mad dream, without justification.' But Muir also recognised that it was 'a historical process incarnated in the flesh and blood of whole peoples', and that it could not stop 'until it has worked itself out'. Its logical end was a state of general wealth and leisure... it was 'our chief earnest of the future'. These judgements which are sage and humane should be borne in mind when one considers the nineteenth century. It is inconceivable that the Industrial Revolution could have been achieved without dreadful hardship, and without creating the gradations of wealth and poverty which were so markedly to be found in Victorian Glasgow. What is perhaps the most distinctive feature of the age is not the indifference shown by many capitalists to the conditions in which their wage-slaves toiled, but the other side of the coin: the encouragement they offered to social improvement, and the public spirit most of them manifested.

The chemical industry showed industrial capitalism at its worst. Since its labour force was largely unskilled, its individual members were expendable. The industry drew on immigrants to the city – in the late 1840s the Irish arrived in Glasgow at the rate of 1000 a week. That level was not maintained, but the combination of agricultural improvements and recurrent agricultural depressions meant that there was always a fresh supply of people crowding into the city in search of work. This kept wage rates down, and profits up; the availability of labour worked to the employers' advantage. Glasgow, like all great and growing cities, was refreshed by waves of incomers who, entering the labour market at the bottom, desperate for work of any kind, made it difficult for workers to combine effectively, and easy for employers to divide and rule unchecked. At the same time these immigrants, ignorant of the habits of urban living, exacerbated social problems, particularly with regard to housing. The easiest money to be made in Victorian Glasgow came from supplying tenement housing to the swelling population.

The tenements were generally put up by speculative builders who financed their construction by taking out bonds or loans payable over a fifteen-year period, and yielding interest generally a point above bank rate. T. C. Smout observes that:

> an enormous number of middle-class people were involved in making a profit from the construction and ownership of the workers' one- and two-roomed houses, ranging from the wealthiest of land speculators, through the solid divisions of the accountants and lawyers, down to the great mass of the petite bourgeoisie – the Free Church clergy and employer craftsmen who were themselves just a generation and an income bracket removed from those whom they housed and whose rents they drew.

Because these bonds were repayable at three months' notice, there was considerable pressure on the builder to construct his houses as soon as possible and then sell them off. This meant that the houses themselves were sometimes shoddily built, but the market was sustained by the continuing demand for new housing created by immigration.

It was not just the manufacturing and commercial magnates who extracted wealth in the form of cheap labour from those at the bottom of the social pyramid; everyone who could scrape some capital together and invest it in housing could draw a rentier income. Accordingly the rapid expansion of the city helped to create a rentier class. In one sense this class was more parasitical than the millionaires, who at least provided work, created opportunities and sought out markets by the exercise of their will, intelligence, energy and imagination. But in another sense their modest investments helped to make the whole structure of industrial capitalism possible, while the dividends they drew were recycled either in consumption or by way of further investment.

The growth of the Glasgow middle class was the result not only of their own labour, but also of their acumen and their eye for an investment. That growth is easily overlooked by social historians if only because it is less well documented than the state of the poor: no Royal or Parliamentary Commissions investigated the condition of the bourgeoisie, and they do not figure prominently in police records – two sources of information about the poor. But the evidence is there nevertheless in stone: in the lines of middle-class terraces in the West End, out towards Kelvinside and Anniesland; in the villas and terraces stretching away south of the river. It is there in the plethora of churches, both of the Established Church and the Free Church, built, generally by public subscription, in all the new parts of the city. Early in the century, before the Disruption, the Church Extension Committee of the Church of Scotland had, at the prompting of Dr Thomas Chalmers, the future leader of the Free Kirk breakaway, but then Minister at St John's in Glasgow, erected 222 new churches in seven years, many in Glasgow. When the split came, Free Kirk congregations were notable for their church-building zeal. This would have been impossible but for the enthusiasm of the middle class; and that enthusiasm would have been vain had they not been growing simultaneously more numerous and richer.

Not all industrial workers were in a condition as wretched as those employed in the chemical business. The Glasgow working class had its own aristocracy, who were to be found in the shipyards. Ships were to become the symbol of Glasgow, the expression of the city's industrial pride. In the rise of the shipbuilding industry Glasgow saw its glory and virtue; its decline after the First World War afflicted the city with a loss of confidence from which it is only perhaps now gradually recovering. But shipbuilding itself represented the apex of Glasgow's achievement; and it depended for its vitality on a concatenation of circumstances.

The first of these was the commercial importance which the city had acquired in the eighteenth century. Then its dominance of the Atlantic trade created a class of men accustomed to seek wealth by trade, and to search out opportunities for expanding that trade. An example of this was the expedition, financed and fitted out by the firm of Alexander and John Downie, which sailed to Ichaboe in 1844 to secure the guano deposits discovered there, a voyage which may be taken as marking the start of the agricultural fertilisers industry in Scotland. By the middle of the century the house of Pollok, Gilmour & Co, trading with the Baltic, was the largest timber-importing establishment in the world. Even early in the Age of Steam, Glasgow was trading all over the world. The growth of the city's trade may be measured by the revenue collected at Glasgow by the Customs & Excise. This rose from just over £8000 in the years after Waterloo to £634,000 in 1847. A notable feature of this increase was that the abolition or reduction of a whole range of duties effected by the Peel Government in 1844 made no difference. Indeed the 1847 figure represents an increase of not much under £100,000 over the two preceding years. This swelling trade gave a natural impetus to shipbuilding.

Commercial activity would have been insufficient by itself to account for Glasgow's greatest industry. Bristol, after all, had long been a great trading port; it never became an important shipbuilding one. Glasgow, however, lay close to the coalfields and ironworks of Lanarkshire, Ayrshire and Stirlingshire. Even when the native iron was exhausted, the availability of coal, and the possibility of cheap imports of iron-ore, enabled Glasgow to flourish as one of the great iron and steel centres of the world; Motherwell, Coatbridge, Gartcosh, Wishaw, Airdrie were steel towns within a few miles of Glasgow. In 1879 they were producing 50,000 tons; forty years later their output had increased to one and a quarter million tons.

The combination of commercial traditions, geographical situation and the availability of iron and steel gave Glasgow great natural advantages. More important, they fostered over a couple of generations a singularly high level of engineering skill. It was not restricted to ships: three of the four largest locomotive building firms in Britain were in Glasgow; they exported railway engines all over the world. Civil engineering followed logically: Tower Bridge in London, the Forth and Tay railway bridges, and most of those of the uncompleted Cape-to-Cairo railway were Glasgow-made.

They came from the firm of Sir William Arrol & Co, Engineers and Bridge-builders. Arrol himself was a figure whose chief interest lies in his representative quality. He was born in Renfrewshire, the son of a cotton-spinner who later became manager of one of J. & P. Coats's mills in Paisley. He served an apprenticeship as a blacksmith before going to work in his early twenties for a Paisley engineering firm. He graduated to the position of foreman, then started his own boiler-making and engineering works in Peel Street, Glasgow. He soon moved into bridge-building and won a contract to build a viaduct over the Clyde at Bothwell for the North British Railway. He devised a method of projecting continuous girders across the river from pier to pier on rollers driven by ratchet bars. It was so successful that he was invited to build the viaduct across the Clyde which carried the Caledonian

Railway into the new Glasgow Central station; to bring this off he had to invent a new type of drilling machine and hydraulic riveting equipment. He was not quite forty, self-educated, working by a mixture of experience and intuition. The next year he was asked to build the Forth Bridge; this involved new technical problems on account of its span and the difficulty of building piers in a rapid and tidal firth. At the same time he was engaged to build the replacement for the Tay bridge which had collapsed in December 1879. A contemporary account, quoted in the *Dictionary of Scottish Business Biography*, of Arrol's week at this time gives a picture of the way he worked:

> Rising at four on Monday morning, he was down at the Dalmarnock Works before five o'clock, busy looking over plans and scheming the details of the work in progress there. A hurried breakfast in a restaurant in Glasgow, on his way to the station, then off to Corstorphine, where a special engine was waiting to run him down to South Queensferry. There he met the various heads of departments engaged in the building of the Forth Bridge, and spent the day – and often the greater part of the night – in arranging, not only how the more important work, but even how many of the minor details should be carried out, and sometimes personally superintending their execution. Early on Tuesday morning he was over at the Tay Bridge, the work of which he carried on in the same way. Back to Glasgow late on Tuesday night, he was down at the Dalmarnock Works by five on Wednesday morning, ready to start the round as before. On Thursday night he started for London to meet the engineers who prepared the plans there, and to discuss with them on Friday the details of any proposed alterations or amendments. Travelling back to Glasgow on Friday night, he was generally at the works till late on Saturday.

Arrol was both organiser and inventor, or deviser. As a skilled hydraulic engineer, he manufactured cranes, jiggers, hoists, lifts, tube-welding and riveting machines. He constructed huge gantries over shipyards such as Beardmore's in Glasgow and Harland & Wolff's in Belfast. With William Foulis, the Glasgow Corporation gas engineer, he invented machines for charging, discharging and cleaning retorts, and supplied them to gas companies throughout Britain.

No man with such a wide range of skills could be described as typical; his genius set him apart from others. Yet the difference was one of scale rather than degree. There were thousands of engineers from similar backgrounds to his in the Glasgow of his day. Like him, most of them had little formal academic training. They worked in the same experimental fashion as he did, even if they failed to match the boldness of his understanding or to equal his comprehensive grasp. Arrol worked fast, so that it has been suggested that 'there was hardly a shipyard or engineering works in Scotland, the North of England or Ireland that he had not done work for'.

In other respects he conforms to accepted patterns of behaviour. He held numerous public appointments, including a directorship of the Glasgow based Union Bank of Scotland (of which Sir Charles Tennant was Chairman) and the managership of the Glasgow Royal Infirmary. His politics were typical too: he was a Liberal until Gladstone brought in the Irish Home Rule Bill in 1886. For Arrol, as for many West of Scotland businessmen, Irish Home Rule seemed a precursor of the break-up of the United Kingdom; it was inconceivable that a man of his imperial interests could approve such a measure. He therefore became one of Joseph Chamberlain's Liberal-Unionist followers, and sat in Parliament for ten years as a Unionist.

The engineering firms of Arrol, Barr & Stroud, and James Howden & Co loomed in the background of the shipyards. They made the ships possible, often indeed making those parts of the ships which the public did not see. Such firms had a good deal in common. They were technically innovative, but their continuing success might depend on individual genius rather than on the creation of a structure which made research and development a priority. Their own innovations were generally responsive, and the tradition they incarnated was later to reveal the defects of the individualistic philosophy which powered Victorian Glasgow. Archibald Barr (1855–1931), one of the founders of Barr & Stroud, Instrument Engineers, might seem an exception to this generalisation. Half a generation younger than Arrol and Howden, he was himself an academic, indeed Regius Professor of Civil Engineering and Mechanics at Glasgow from 1889 to 1913; as such, he recognised the value of theoretical training, and introduced sandwich courses at the University for undergraduates of engineering and applied science; he persuaded local firms to send able apprentices to the University. But if he was an exception, his example was not widely followed. In the twentieth century one explanation frequently advanced for Glasgow's loss of leadership in the field of technology and applied science would be its ingrained preference for rule-of-thumb empiricism, and its apparent reluctance to build on pure research.

In the Victorian Age, however, Glasgow was one of the workshops of the world, and its great ships the city's most glorious work. Since Henry Bell had launched the first steamship on the Clyde in 1812 the advance of the industry had been constant. The secret of success lay in engineering superiority; the successive stages in marine engine design associated with John Elder, James Howden, A. C. Kirk at Fairfields and Walter Brock at

Denny of Dumbarton secured world leadership for the Clyde. In percentage terms the peak was probably reached by 1870 when 70 per cent of all iron vessels and two-thirds of all steamships were built there. Yet even these figures are less impressive than the revelation that in 1914 the Clyde launched one-third of British tonnage, 18 per cent of world tonnage and more than the total shipbuilding production of either the United States or Germany. Some forty firms were engaged in shipbuilding on the river.

Shipbuilding was very much a family affair. This was as true in the yards as in the boardrooms, though it is naturally easier to identify family succession and connections among the owners. So, for example, there were seven generations of Stephens connected with the firm that became best known as Alexander Stephen & Son; four of Connells; three of Lithgows; three of Dennys; three of Gilchrists at Barclay Curle. No doubt there were some disadvantages attached to this dynastic succession; there were also benefits. Men associated with a firm and a yard from birth recognised obligations which at least mollified the sharpness of capitalist business logic. Sir James Lithgow (1883–1952), who, with his yonger brother Henry, took full control of the family firm on their father's death in 1908, followed a policy which he had established: not to take dividends, but to keep resources within the company, and from large reserves contrive to maintain employment in their yards even in periods of depression. They were able to do this only because of the capital accumulated by previous generations, and it may be argued that this paternalistic attitude inhibited the formation of habits of thought which might better have secured the industry's future. Nevertheless it humanised what were otherwise harsh relationships; it played its part in binding all classes in Glasgow together in a recognisable identity, of which indeed all classes were proud. David Kirkwood, the Labour MP, tells a story in his autobiography, *My Life of Revolt* (1935), of an incident in his time during the First World War as a shop-steward at Beardmore's, the shipbuilders and armament-makers, which illustrates the mollifying effect of paternalism. A craftsman had misjudged cutting a crank by one-thousandth of an inch and as a result had wasted materials worth one thousand pounds. Beardmore himself was summoned to give judgement. He stood over the bench, a cigar in his mouth, looking at the worker and what he had done. Then he asked the manager: 'Can we make another?' 'Yes, sir.' 'Then get the thing done.' The incident was over, the matter closed. Kirkwood added his reflection: 'To err is human, to forgive divine.'

If the owners felt themselves to be gods, the working men in the shipyards were themselves servants of an impersonal God. Kipling's engineer MacAndrew saw 'predestination in the stroke o' yon connecting-rod'.

There was a mystique of the shipyards. Whereas in other industries labour had a degrading effect, shipyard workers could feel pride in their work. The dissociation of their activity from a finished product, characteristic of most sorts of factory labour, was unknown to them. They were proud of their status as skilled craftsmen, 'time-served' men; it was inconceivable that they should experience alienation. They were worked hard, sometimes, when a contract had to be fulfilled against time, terribly hard, driven on by foremen, who had great authority, whose word was law as regards continued employment. They knew periods of unemployment when trade was slack or orders low, but they were never negligible; they could not be disregarded and they were in no doubt as to their own worth.

Trade Union activity was at a relatively low level on the Clyde before the First World War. There were several reasons for this. The foremen and skilled workers, whose employment was more or less secure, owed vertical loyalties to their firm more strongly than horizontal loyalties to class. The semi-skilled and labourers were accustomed to being laid off and to moving from yard to yard as work was offered. The first group had little reason to wish to make common cause with the second. They regarded themselves as the aristocrats of the labour movement. This meant that in important respects they shared their employers' ideology, seeing themselves as individuals and believing as firmly as their employers that the individual had the ability to shape his own life; that success was the natural reward of skill, sobriety, character and industry. Their religious beliefs reinforced this. Nothing in their experience contradicted this habit of thought. A skilled worker in Glasgow, born at any time in Queen Victoria's reign, could see around him the fruits of individual enterprise. His own living conditions had improved immeasurably in the course of his working life. His children, at least after the Education Act of 1872, were assured of free schooling, and all over the city he could see schools being built by the Parish Boards. The Exhibitions of 1888 and 1901 confirmed his instinctive view that he was a citizen of the greatest industrial city in the world, a place of which he could feel justly proud, its achievements the work of men like himself.

Kirkwood in his autobiography told a story which reads like a biblical parable. It concerned two groups of boys: one made up of members of the Good Templars temperance association, of which he was one; the other a set whom he called 'The Jolly Twelve'.

We met for lectures, concerts, socials and the rest of it. We also went to night school. We had no money. 'The Jolly Twelve' had money from their mothers. They had the evenings to themselves, went into Glasgow and came home late, often the worse for drink, when they would become noisy, swearing young men. They called it 'seeing life'. Of the eleven of 'The Jolly Twelve' none lived beyond thirty-six, and eight killed themselves. I know of none that left children, but one committed suicide a week before his son was born. Of the eleven of the other group, all are living except one (who died at sixty-three). Everyone prospered and their families prosper too.

The little homily was intended as a warning against drink and loose living. It stands equally well as a statement of the serious young Glasgow working-man's sense of the possibilities open to him. Everyone who acquired a skill and lived a careful and industrious life could succeed. The capitalist ethos was to be found even among socialists such as Kirkwood. Life was governed by character and will, rather than by economic laws. There was, it seemed, a free market in life.

The contrast between the shipyard workers and those condemned to the hell of the St Rollox works or White's chemical factory called such confidence in question. The shipyard workers were fortunate; they were not only accomplices in industrial expansion; they might even be called partners. They shared in its successes. But there were other workers who were involuntary accomplices, and Industrialism's victims. The test for the whole society would come when the market turned against Glasgow. Then it would be seen what resources individualism truly retained. Till then, however, the emergence of a stratum of skilled workers who did well out of the system not only ameliorated its hardships but seemed to justify them. Even more important it contributed to the homogeneity of Glasgow, to its distinctive and self-reliant character.

1a *Above:* A seventeenth century engraving of Glasgow seen from the north-east.

1b *Below:* Broomielaw in the eighteenth century

2 Lansdowne Church and the first and second bridges over the Kelvin in 1870

3a *Above:* Paddle-steamers *Iona, Benmore* and *Daniel Adamson* at Broomielaw in 1895

3b *Below:* Glasgow University, 1906

4 *Above:* George Square looking north-west, 1870

5 *Opposite:* A close off the Saltmarket, 1868

7 *Above:* Open sewers flowed freely through some of Glasgow's slums (1910)

6 *Opposite:* A staircase in a tenement building in Nicholson Street in the Gorbals, 1950.

8a *Above:* The H.L.I. (Highland Light Infantry) march down Sauchiehall Street into
Renfield Street en route for France (1915)

8b *Below:* Children protesting at the rent rises imposed by landlords in 1915

CHAPTER FIVE

POLITICAL GLASGOW

Early nineteenth-century Glasgow was a Whig city. This was not necessarily reflected in Parliamentary representation, for it shared its single member with the burghs of Renfrew, Rutherglen and Dumbarton, till the Reform Act of 1832 rectified the situation, and gave the city two members, still an inadequate reflection of its size and importance. Nevertheless, even before then, the great merchant Kirkman Finlay had been elected in 1812 – the first native Glaswegian MP for almost a hundred years. Finlay, in alliance with fellow Whigs, James Ewing and James Oswald – all three particularly rich men – campaigned for liberation of trade from monopolistic restrictions; his especial target was the East India Company. This was not surprising in view of his own ambitions to trade with the East.

If Glasgow's Parliamentary representation was undemocratic, the city's own government also ill reflected the changes that were taking place. Until the enactment of the Municipal Reform Bill of 1833 (two years earlier than the corresponding English measure) membership of the Glasgow Corporation was restricted to the Merchants' and Trades' Houses; it was self-elected, proceeding by the principle of co-option. The Whig reforms established a franchise of £10 householders, and divided the old royal burgh into five wards, from which thirty councillors were elected; two ex-officio members were added from the Merchants' and Trades' Houses. Thirteen years later a new Act extended the authority of the Corporation over suburban districts which had been built over beyond the old territory of the royal burgh. The number of councillors was increased to fifty, and the number of wards to sixteen.

The corporation had the right of presentment to nine of the ten city parishes. It appointed all the masters in the High School, and awarded bursaries there and at the University. Its turnover in the 1840s was put at £200,000 a year. The 1833 Act had given it the authority to raise rates for lighting, cleaning, water supply, draining and police. Not, however, till an Act of 1862 revived the authority of the old Dean of Guild Court does it seem to have exercised control over building. Then it began to insist on certain standards; one result of this was that a four-storey building in Glasgow came to cost almost half as much again as a similar one in London. This was to the advantage of the appearance of the city, but it increased the rent payable on working-class property. Since, in general, the Scottish working class were not prepared, or not able, to spend as high a proportion of their income on housing, as their counterparts in England, this contributed to the overcrowding of Glasgow by helping to force families into single-room dwellings.

City politics operate on both a local and national scale. In the 1840s the national element was more conspicuous. Glasgow was strongly in favour of the repeal of the Corn Laws, the great issue of the decade following Parliamentary reform. The business community in Glasgow, who dominated the Corporation, were keen supporters of Free Trade. In April 1841 Lord Cockburn, who as Solicitor-General had drawn up the Scottish Reform Bill, wrote of a public meeting in Glasgow 'where principles of commercial freedom were expounded by our greatest merchants of all sects', even the Conservative leader, Sir James Campbell, being in favour of repeal. Their support of Free Trade was not disinterested. The Corn Laws kept the price of bread high, and so compelled manufacturers to pay wages which would be high enough to keep their workers safe from starvation; if the price of bread dropped, they would find it easier to keep wage-costs down.

The repeal was effected, breaking the old Tory Party, and confirming Scotland and Glasgow in allegiance to the Whigs who were now transforming themselves into Liberals. It did not prove an immediate cure for the Depression which led the decade to be called the 'Hungry Forties'. Chartists, who demanded fundamental political reforms, found great support in Glasgow where the Depression had temporarily driven unemployment to unprecedented levels. In April 1848 – the Year of Revolution on the Continent – a crowd, wildly estimated at anything between 40,000 and 100,000 assembled on Glasgow Green where a few weeks earlier the police had fired into a throng of the unemployed. But the movement died away as prosperity returned in the 1850s. It left a legacy, however, in the renewed willingness of the working class to organise themselves in various voluntary organisations, which would in time make it clear that they were fit to be trusted with civic responsibility.

The more immediate consequence of the urban unrest of the 1840s was the impetus which it gave to municipal activity. *Laissez-faire*, it was made clear, might be highly desirable, indeed essential, in commercial and industrial affairs, but that it also created problems of urban living, which it made no effort to solve, was now apparent. Moreover, these problems threatened the stability of institutions and the security of the middle-classes. If up to 100,000 disaffected proletarians could foregather on Glasgow Green, what would it take to turn them into a mob of Parisian ferocity? The European revolutions of 1848 were a warning; the Glasgow slums were a reproach. Policy, self-interest and humanity all pointed the same way: control and reform were both necessary. Fortunately, they were not distinct. Control indeed was a species of social reform; reform could not be effected without the assumption of control.

A Corporation composed largely of businessmen addressed itself to the question of correcting the abuses of industrialism without, they hoped, impairing its spirit or diluting its energy. The first great project was the already-mentioned provision of a hygienic public water supply. Its success was immediately evident: when cholera returned to Scotland in 1865–6 only fifty-three deaths were recorded in Glasgow. The epidemic was altogether less severe than its predecessor, and only 400 people died of it in Scotland; but in the earlier outbreak Glasgow had had 4000 of Scotland's 6000 fatalities. A drop from 66 per cent of the Scottish total to a mere 13 per cent justified the Corporation's investment.

Assertions of the municipality's right, indeed duty, to exercise control came thick and fast. A Medical Officer of Health was appointed in 1863. The previous year the Corporation obtained the right to regulate the number of people who might live in a house: metal plates were fixed to walls of houses of a certain size stating how many people might sleep there – this was called 'ticketing'. The police were granted powers of search. Within twenty years one in seven Glaswegians lived in ticketed houses.

The Glasgow Improvement Act was passed in 1866. This allowed slum clearance, though it made no provision for re-housing; it would be another twenty years before the Corporation began to build houses of its own. Nevertheless the combination of ticketing and compulsory slum clearance contributed to the elimination of the very worst properties, some of which had already been cleared to make way for railway lines and termini. If succeeding generations were still to gaze in horror at what remained, or what replaced these old properties, that was as much a measure of the infernal scale of the problem as of the Corporations's failure to solve it.

A city, it began to appear, could be treated, and perhaps should be treated, as a great nobleman ordered his estates. It was susceptible to rational control and planned improvement. The city's gas companies were municipalised in 1867, and the price of gas halved. The Corporation took on itself the responsibility of lighting courts and tenements as well as the main streets; more households were connected to the mains than in any other city in the world. Ten years later tramlines were laid; in 1894 the tramway companies were taken over by the Corporation; and the trams ran at a profit. A fever hospital was built in 1869, baths and wash-houses established in 1878, even a municipal laundry service five years later. In 1901 the Corporation created a telephone network.

Nor was this all. Spiritual, moral and intellectual elevation was also provided: in the Art Gallery in Kelvingrove, in the People's Palace on Glasgow Green, by municipal concerts and public parks.

An anonymous English writer summed up the phenomenon that was Glasgow in the *Fortnightly Review* (Jan. 1903):

> In Glasgow a citizen may live in a municipal house; he may walk along the municipal street, or ride on the municipal tramcar and watch the municipal dustcart collecting the refuse which is to be used to fertilise the municipal farm. Then he may turn into the municipal market, buy a steak from an animal killed in the municipal slaughterhouse, and cook it by the municipal gas stove. For his recreation he can choose among municipal libraries, municipal art galleries, and municipal music in municipal parks. Should he fall ill, he can ring up his doctor on the municipal telephone, or he may be taken to the municipal hospital in the municipal ambulance by a municipal policeman. Should he be so unfortunate as to get on fire, he will be put out by the municipal fireman, using municipal water; after which he will, perhaps, forego the enjoyment of using the municipal bath, though he may find it necessary to get a new suit in the municipal old clothes market...

Or send his old one, perhaps, to the municipal laundry.

Glasgow was not alone in assuming control of urban life or even in the assumption of the duty to provide for the welfare of its citizens. Joseph Chamberlain was doing the same thing in Birmingham in the 1860s, and Baron Haussmann in Paris. But Glasgow went further, and became a model. In the last decades of the nineteenth century, it regularly received deputations from American cities – from Chicago, New York, Boston and Detroit – all seeking to learn the management of an industrial city. It looks to a later generation like Socialism; it didn't seem so to the men who created the system, and they would have been horrified at the attribution of the word 'Socialist' to their policies. Rather, their principles, as Michael Fry has suggested in his political history of modern Scotland, *Patronage and Principle* (1987):

> had a startling similarity to those of Scotland's defunct ecclesiastical constitution, long vainly upheld by the Free Church – of which it was

perhaps no accident that two outstanding Lord Provosts of the period, Sir Samuel Chisholm and Sir Daniel Macaulay Stevenson, were members. It accorded to the state only the duty of providing the wherewithal to the institutions catering for the people's welfare, which otherwise acted in the freedom they chose for themselves. Glasgow Corporation had a visionary ambition to create an ideal industrial society where the energy of capitalism and the morals of the citizen would be brought into harmony through strict regulation. That gave social control to the bourgeoisie but offered much to the workers... The Corporation's policies reinforced their assent to a system in which clashes of capital and labour were deliberately defused.

The Corporation was authoritarian, like the Kirk. But, like the Kirk, its authoritarianism was in the first place a matter of setting limits, within which the individual was expected – in the moral sphere, required – to make his own life, and assume responsibility for his own well-being. It might point the way to Socialism: its recipe of limited social control in the interests of welfare and efficiency could be transmuted into social engineering and the theory of bureaucratic superiority. But the true heir of the nineteenth-century Glasgow Corporation was to be found among the Tory paternalists. This was Walter Elliot, from Glasgow Academy and the University of Glasgow, later Member of Parliament for Kelvingrove, who, in *Toryism and the Twentieth Century* (1927), proposed what was in effect the adaptation of the principles of the Glasgow Corporation on a national scale.

At the time the Corporation was Liberal, not Tory. The principle of Free Trade was dear to Glasgow. The city imported food and raw materials; it exported manufactured goods. It associated Conservatism with the landed interest and the retention of out-dated privileges. Things began to change with Gladstone's Irish Home Rule Bill of 1886. This was unpopular for two reasons. First, it threatened the Empire on which Glasgow depended. Second, its sympathy for the aspirations of a largely Catholic nation aroused sectarian opposition in Glasgow. The city depended on the Catholic Irish for much of its cheap labour, but the native Protestant working-class feared and resented the Irish, whom they jealously excluded from employment, whenever possible. Moreover, many of the Irish immigrants were themselves Protestants from Ulster, hostile to Gladstone's proposals and ready to play the Orange card. Working-class Unionism therefore became a feature of the city's political life. Eventually, as the Liberal Unionists were absorbed into the Conservative Party, the Orange vote became a Tory one. It prevented Glasgow politics from dividing absolutely on class lines till it weakened, and then virtually disappeared in the 1960s.

Local politics eschewed party divisions, but the ethos of the Corporation was Liberal Unionist by the end of the century. This need not have implied support for the Conservative Party. A Liberal Imperialist wing existed, ready to ditch Irish Home Rule. Its leader was the Earl of Rosebery, Prime Minister from 1894 to 1896. Rosebery preached the attractive, if vague, doctrine of 'efficiency'. Its model might have been Glasgow Corporation which already practised what he preached: paternalism and practical reform directed from above.

Yet, whatever movements there were between the three political groupings, movements further blurred by the split within the Conservative and Unionist parties over Joseph Chamberlain's campaign for tariff reform (1903–6), this model was already out of date. A new force was entering the closed world of Parliamentary politics; this was the rise of organised labour. This would change politics in the twentieth century; it would change Glasgow too. Indeed the city's image would alter completely within a quarter of a century. From being an admired model of bourgeois Liberal efficiency, it would become the place where the British Revolution threatened to erupt. That the change was one of image rather than reality is immaterial; cities are always to some extent what they are thought to be. Nineteenth-century Glasgow was neither as efficient nor as rational as it seemed; that image, nevertheless, helped to promote an appreciation of its greatness. Likewise, the Clyde never flowed as Red as it was thought to do; but the myth of Red Clydeside contributed to the loss of confidence in Glasgow, and the perception of a grievously troubled city.

CHAPTER SIX

A FEAST OF CULTURE

Between 1870 and 1914 Glasgow reached its apogee. Whatever its social problems, it was one of the richest and most splendid of European cities. Whatever the failures of its governors to solve these problems, they were ambitious and benevolent men, fully conscious of their duty to the city. This period, therefore, saw two great international exhibitions, both held in Kelvingrove Park, in 1888 and 1901; the second of these drew an attendance of eleven and a half million, many people visiting several times. It was dedicated to art, industry and science. It brought gondolas to the Kelvin and celebrated Glasgow's own achievements in its Machinery Hall and its Industrial Hall. It represented a stupendous display of confidence and pride in Glasgow's achievement.

It was a time of great public building. The University had been transplanted to Gilmorehill some twenty years earlier and the greatest architect of mid-nineteenth-century Glasgow, Alexander Thomson, died in 1875. Sir George Gilbert Scott wrote of the University of Glasgow:

> I adopted a style which I may call my own invention having already initiated it at the Albert Institute in Dundee (1865–7). It is simply a thirteenth- or fourteenth-century secular style, with the addition of certain Scottish features peculiar in that country in the sixteenth century.

The site was an inspired choice and the native stone has weathered in such a way as to make it one of the greatest and most magnificent of Glasgow's buildings. However much one may regret the move of the University from its old site in the High Street, no one can disparage the building at Gilmorehill, and to approach it across Kelvingrove Park or from University Avenue on a winter afternoon is to be reminded that architecture can have a dramatic function. That was Thomson's characteristic too. His 'Greek' sobriquet implies a limitation which the body of his work denies. He did not employ only Greek motifs; he was, as befitted the architect in a city such as Glasgow, eclectic in his choice of style and material. In his best work the dramatic effect makes consideration of the source of his style irrelevant.

One paradox of Glasgow is that the city, notorious for former slums and present-day bleak housing-estates, also possesses more parks and open spaces, proportionate to its size, than any other city in Europe. That is the result of the determination of its nineteenth-century Corporation of Liberal businessmen to provide for the recreational and cultural needs of their fellow citizens. Nowhere was this desire more evident than in the building of the People's Palace on Glasgow Green. This was opened in 1898. The Earl of Rosebery, performing the opening ceremony, hoped that it would become 'a palace of pleasure and imagination around which the people may place their affections and which may give them a home on which their memory may rest'. It had been a long time in the making, for it was twenty years since the Glasgow Public Parks, Museums & Galleries Act had empowered the Corporation to spend public money on such things, but the passing of that Act had itself been a significant declaration of the City Fathers' determination to provide for cultural welfare.

The case for the People's Palace was put forward by Councillor Robert Crawford in a paper delivered to the Ruskin Society in 1891. There could hardly have been a more suitable audience, for Crawford's recognition of the importance of culture in the lives of ordinary citizens was influenced by Ruskin's own writings. Crawford happened to be Chairman of the Health Committee as well as of the Committee for Galleries and Museums, and he argued that public health and municipal art were connected. If it was the city's duty to provide for the physical well-being of its citizens, then a similar duty pertained where spiritual refreshment was concerned. Some people might argue that the working class had shown no interest in art; but the proper way to create such an interest was to provide the opportunity. It hadn't demanded municipal baths, but had happily used them when provided.

Crawford was supported by one of his colleagues, Bailie Bilsland, an advocate of free libraries, free ferries, free museums, free recreation grounds and more public parks. In a speech at the opening ceremony, he said:

> The general idea is that the permanent collections to be formed should relate to the history and industries of the city, and that some space should be set apart for special sectional exhibitions to be held from time to time. While primarily serving as a conservatory and a place of attraction during the shorter days, the Winter Gardens portion has been designed and arranged to serve also as a hall where musical performances can be given to large audiences. One element of originality in the way of municipal enterprise that

can be claimed for this institution lies in the combination, practically under one roof, of a museum, a picture gallery, winter gardens and music hall. So far as we are aware, no municipality in the kingdom has provided an institution combining all these features.

The Winter Gardens were said to offer a 'treasure-house of the beautiful in shrub and flower'.

There could have been no more suitable place to build the People's Palace than Glasgow Green, for it was old Glasgow's place of recreation, debate, demonstrations, even battle; it was to Glasgow what the Forum was to Ancient Rome, and perhaps more, for the Forum did not offer the same spectacle of *rus in urbe*. It was also appropriate that the People's Palace should offer an education in both art and science, for Glasgow had been made by science, and it was science which had made the flowering of art possible there. Moreover, it was while walking on the Green that James Watt had conceived the idea which changed the history of the world:

> I had gone to take a walk on a fine Sabbath afternoon, early in 1765. I had entered the Green by the gate at the foot of Charlotte Street, and had passed the old washing house. I was thinking upon the engine at the time, and had gone as far as the herd's house, when the idea came into my mind that, as steam was an elastic body, it would rush into a vacuum, and if a communication were made between the cylinder and an exhausted vessel, it would rush into it and might be condensed without cooling the cylinder. I had not walked further than the golf-house when the whole thing was arranged in my mind.

On the bicentenary of his inspiration, a large boulder was placed at the spot on the Green where the Industrial Revolution was conceived.

The culture of Glasgow has never evinced the separation between – even opposition of – art and science said to be characteristic of modern Britain. This was partly because of the generalist tradition of Scottish education, always stoutly defended in the University of Glasgow, which required students to take courses which included at least one arts and one science subject. But it was also because it was impossible for anyone in Glasgow, whatever his inclinations, to divorce himself from the scientific and technological source of the city's wealth. It was impossible to live in Glasgow and not be aware of the shipyards; the artist Muirhead Bone wrote of 'the engineering skies of Glasgow'.

Accordingly, Glasgow was as proud of its great scientists as of any of its great men, and there was widespread approval when the greatest of its nineteenth-century scientists, William Thomson, took as his title, on being made a peer, the name of Kelvin, after the little river that flows through the park below the University.

Kelvin was Professor of Mathematics and Natural Philosophy in the University for fifty-three years; he had matriculated there in 1834 at the age of ten and, when he was sixteen, won the University medal for an essay 'On the Figure of the Earth'. On the occasion of his jubilee as Professor, the University held a celebratory exhibition. The library was filled with a display of his inventions. Two thousand guests attended. A telegram of congratulation was dispatched to him from the library. Travelling by way of Newfoundland and New York to the coast of California and back across the Atlantic, it returned to him in seven and a half minutes. It was Kelvin himself who had invented the submarine cable, and the telegram was proof of the practicality of his genius. There could hardly have been a more suitable demonstration of how the nineteenth century had changed Glasgow than that gathering in the University library, or, even more strikingly, of how Glasgow had helped change the world.

Kelvin was as practical as any Glasgow businessman; indeed he was a Glasgow businessman himself. He had personally supervised the laying of the first Atlantic cable just as Sir William Arrol would oversee the construction of his great bridges. More than that, realising that the practical application of science depended on the quality of the instruments available, he not only invented and developed instruments, he manufactured them also. He went into partnership with James White, a maker of optical instruments, and the firm of Kelvin & White manufactured and marketed instruments and devices for electrical and optical measuring, telegraph transmitting and navigational aids. In the 1890s the firm employed 200 skilled technicians. The divorce between the pure and applied branches of science would have made no sense to him.

In his industry, versatility, imagination and intellect, Kelvin was one of the greatest of eminent Victorians. He was also, in important respects, characteristic of his age and city. A member of the Free Kirk, he would open his lecture with a prayer; expounding the laws of thermodynamics to a class of young men studying for an Ordinary Degree, he was unravelling the mystery of a benevolent creation. He refused several offers of a Chair at Cambridge; nothing could tempt him away from Glasgow. His was a unified character, and in this he mirrored his city: he strove to maintain links between science, philosophy and the humanities, believing that he had derived great benefit himself from his study of the Classics – at the age of twelve he had won a prize for his translation of Lucian's *Dialogue of the Gods*. It was appropriate that, from the University, he could watch the building of the great municipal Art Gallery & Museum across the park.

There was a confident sense of common identity among Glaswegians. It derived partly from shared experience, partly from the pervasive feeling that they were all partners in success. The wealth and splendour of Glasgow grew ever more visible, keeping pace with the expansion of the British Empire in which Glasgow played so significant, so fruitful, a part. In this imperial sunshine the middle class, especially, flourished. The West End of the city was built over with rows of handsome terraces, branching out from Great Western Road; beyond the slums that crowded the river on the south side were acres of substantial villas and luxuriant gardens. Many of the richer bourgeoisie moved beyond the city to Helensburgh or Kilcreggan, Troon or Largs, depending on the railway and the ferry to bring them in to their offices. They bought lavishly; conspicuous expenditure had become a Glasgow characteristic. Much of it went on furniture, furnishings, *objets d'art* and paintings; the great magpie Sir William Burrell, shipowner and art-collector, whose bequest to the city was at last to be realised in the 1980s thanks to the generous gift of the Pollok estate by the Maxwell-Macdonald family, differed from his fellow citizens in the scale and magnificence of his collecting, but his enthusiasm was typical of thousands.

It was natural for merchants, professional men, manufacturers and managers to commission portraits of their wives, and daughters, and accordingly around the turn of the century as many as two hundred portrait painters might be found working professionally in Glasgow. More important was the group of painters known affectionately as the Glasgow Boys who came together about 1881 when W.Y. Macgregor started holding life-classes in his studio at 134 Bath Street. The Glasgow Boys never constituted a school, and there is dispute as to how many there were, or whether certain particular painters were truly associated with them, but the work of the best of them – James Guthrie, John Lavery, E. A. Walton, Arthur Melville, George Henry and E. A. Hornel and Macgregor himself – has a fresh directness and spontaneity that are wholly delightful. They all have what Stuart Park – another of the Boys – demanded of flower-paintings: 'adequate carrying power'. They found a ready market for their work among their fellow citizens, and many of the best examples now hang in the gallery at Kelvingrove. The rooms devoted to the Glasgow Boys there offer much of interest to the social historian as well as aesthetic delight.

They were fortunate to work when Glasgow's confidence had not yet been undermined. There were few signs of the city's decline evident in 1900, though historians, with the advantage of retrospection, may detect them, and see, like Sydney Checkland, what was hidden from contemporaries:

> The evolution of the economy of Glasgow between 1875 and 1914 is a classic example of the limitation of business-time horizons. It illustrates also the tendency, where circumstances have permitted, to develop a high level of mutually confirming specialisations, to press the advantages of such a situation, to be blind to warnings of its precariousness, and to seek opiates that will allow it to continue. In this way it was possible to ignore the erosion of the fundamental basis of the Clydeside economy brought about by changes in demand, the rise of foreign rivals, and the refusal of other nations to continue in a state of dependence upon British suppliers.

There is no indication of approaching crisis in the luminous landscapes and interiors, the delicate and assured portraits, the still lifes that speak of the comfort and refinement of bourgeois living; the Glasgow Boys seem now to belong to a still, perfect moment of a late summer afternoon; yet their spontaneity and naturalism suggests it might last for ever.

Late Victorian Glasgow produced no novelist either to give a hint of what might be wrong or insubstantial in that society; not even a Galsworthy to anatomise Glasgow's Forsytes, far less a Kafka to call the whole apparatus into question, or a Musil to indicate the discrepancies between appearance and reality, to show how this rich and beautiful world rested on rotting foundations. In retrospect this failure to produce a novelist capable of doing justice to the extraordinary phenomenon of Victorian Glasgow seems stranger than the blindness to the future which Checkland has identified. In fact, if we seek some artistic premonition of decline, we must look to the career of Charles Rennie Mackintosh.

Mackintosh was born in Glasgow in 1868, the son of a police super-intendent, and was educated at Allan Glen's School before entering an apprenticeship with the firm of John Hutcheson. He attended evening classes at the School of Art which, under the directorship of Francis Newbery, a friend of many of the Glasgow Boys, provided an intelligent and stimulating ambience. In 1889 Mackintosh became a partner in the firm of Honeyman & Keppie, and it was for them that he drew the designs which won the competition for the new School of Art in 1896. Before then, he had expressed his view (with a nod to W.R. Lethaby) about the appropriate function of architecture in Scotland then in two lectures to the Glasgow Architectural Association:

> All great and living architecture has been the direct expression of the needs and beliefs of man at the time of its creation, and now if we would have great architecture created, this should still be so .... It is absurd to think it is the

duty of the modern architect to make believe that he is living five, six hundred, or even a thousand years ago.

On the other hand, with this expression of faith in the validity of Modernism went an understanding of the value of tradition, and especially of national tradition:

> The last of the historic claims of this architecture to which I will call your attention is that it is the national architecture of our own country and of our forefathers. All I mean to urge is the simple fact that, by whatever members of our family of nations it was shared, it was nevertheless the architecture of our own country, just as much Scotch as we are ourselves – as indigenous to our country as our wild flowers, our family name, our customs or our political constitution ...

He achieved this synthesis of Modernism with national tradition in his School of Art. It was unmistakably new, equally unmistakably Scottish. The site was difficult; he made it serve his purpose. The massive east wall may remind one of a Scottish castle; yet it is an utterly urban building, and one quite without any reminiscent nostalgia for another age. It is a building which says: here we are, now, and proud of it. His biographer, Thomas Howarth, called it 'the synthesis of traditional craftsmanship and twentieth-century engineering' – like the great ships which made 'Clyde-built' a synonym for quality. It was the first important example of the new movement in Europe, and the example was eventually influential, but on the Continent of Europe rather than in Scotland and England.

Mackintosh had other commissions which allowed him to display his genius: Queen's Cross Church (now the headquarters of the Charles Rennie Mackintosh Society), built in a Glasgow Style Gothic with a tower inspired by a medieval one at Merriot, Somerset, and two elegant large houses: Windyhill in Kilmacolm and The Hill House, Helensburgh. Of these Sir Nikolaus Pevsner wrote: 'They are in their general outline descendants of the Scottish manor-houses ... but their combination of windows, chimney stacks and oriels is of a subtle irregularity, at first appearing arbitrary, but then revealing itself as most sensitively placed and scaled – very much what Le Corbusier did in his later works, but without the brutality.' Then there were Scotland Street School (1904–6) and the various commissions for Miss Cranston's tea-rooms in Buchanan Street, Argyle Street, Ingram Street and, most notably, The Willow tea-rooms in Sauchiehall Street, where Mackintosh and his wife Margaret Macdonald were actively encouraged to design everything, from furniture to cutlery. But after the completion in 1907–9 of the dramatic west wing of the School of Art, there were no new major commissions in Glasgow, with the exception of designs for the furniture and decorations for the Dug-Out during the First World War.

What had gone wrong? It was to some extent a personal failure in that, for one reason or another, he had begun to drink heavily. But Robert Macleod has put his finger on a stronger, professional reason:

> Problems of accounting (and accountability), of contract law, of specification and information were all constricting the artistic autonomy that the architect tended to feel – particularly if he read Ruskin – was his due. Within this more and more impersonal working framework, where every party to the building enterprise was constrained by documentation, it became a continuous battle for Mackintosh – and others of the same persuasion – to manipulate, refine and improve their projects as they developed.

At any rate, Mackintosh lost, for the moment, the ability to concentrate and when his firm entered a competition to design Jordanhill Demonstration School, his drawings were found to be impractical. Some of his corridors ended – like his career – in mid-air. In 1913 he and Margaret left Glasgow for Suffolk and London, and never worked there again.

Yet his 'failure' was not only personal. A Viennese magazine had stated in 1906: 'It is indeed a great delight to oppose an all-powerful enemy, and that is precisely why Charles Rennie Mackintosh is working in Glasgow.' It was, perhaps, a delight more easily experienced at a distance. It is impossible not to see in Glasgow's failure to make full use of the talents of one of its greatest architects a hint of the city's impending decline; the contrast between the boundless opportunities offered Thomson and the few that came Mackintosh's way is marked; it was as if the city was reluctant to commit itself to the new century.

After the First World War Glasgow began to replace its worst slums with some of the worst architecture in Europe. The man who might have brought a civilising imagination to this work was painting watercolours in the south of France. After the Second World War came the tower-blocks, examples of architectural barbarism, evidence of a broken tradition, of a lack of awareness of the function of buildings – though the highly imaginative work of Gillespie Kidd & Coia, in particular, is deserving of praise. Could any of that architectural 'mismanagement' have been avoided if Mackintosh's career had not been broken, if he had been encouraged to work fruitfully in Glasgow? (His later designs for work in Chelsea and Northampton showed that his creative imagination was certainly not liverish.) However much Mackintosh failed himself, Glasgow failed him too; in failing him, it also failed itself.

CHAPTER SEVEN

OUTSIDERS

R eflective views of a city are often best given by those who do not fully belong there, who have other standards by which to measure its life, and who find strange what natives accept as natural. Three who offer such glimpses of Glasgow are Gilbert Murray, John Buchan and Edwin Muir.

Murray became Professor of Greek in the University in 1889 and held the post for ten years. He was only twenty-three when elected, rather to his own surprise. The appointment was made on the recommendation of his predecessor, Sir Richard Jebb, the greatest Greek scholar of his generation; it was opposed by G.G. Ramsay, the Professor of Latin, who considered Murray much too young, and said that his politics were 'pernicious' (he was a Liberal) and his views on religion 'deplorable' (he was an agnostic). Doubts were expressed by the Corporation's representatives among the Electors of the University, who were, as Murray put it, 'ready to admit knowledge of Greek, but point out that none of my testimonials says that I come from a respectable family. They made a great bother about this and said it was a "significant omission".' He repaired it by soliciting testimonials from his future father-in-law, the Earl of Carlisle, and from James Bryce, the Glaswegian historian of the Holy Roman Empire. Thus fortified, he was duly elected, his religious doubts not proving a deterrent; he was only required to pledge himself 'not to attempt to undermine in any Professorial lectures the principles of the Confession of Westminster, whatever they may be'.

Though Murray would later be prominent in politics, as a Liberal who opposed the Boer War, and then as one of the chief supporters of the League of Nations, his interest in Glasgow was wholly concentrated on the University. His background made this foreign to him. Born in Australia, brought up and educated in London, and then at Oxford, he was quite ignorant of what to expect. He had no knowledge of Scotland, let alone Glasgow, for his own branch of the Murray family had settled in Ireland in the seventeenth century – one ancestor had fought in the Battle of the

Boyne, where William of Orange became the 'King Billy' of Protestant heroic mythology, and his own great-grandfather had been a member of Wolfe Tone's United Irishmen, and had lost a leg in the Rising of 1798. Moreover, Murray was set further apart from his professional colleagues by his marriage to Lady Mary Howard, whose upbringing at Castle Howard did not exactly fit her for life at No 5, The University. Finally, both Murrays were teetotallers, and keen supporters of the Temperance Movement. This had many members in Glasgow, where the Scottish Band of Hope Union had been founded in 1871, with William Quarrier, the founder of the City Orphanage and the Quarrier's Homes, as its first Chairman. It was less popular in the University, and Murray was advised by one of his Oxford friends to remember that 'if there is a thing in the Scotch which is incurable it is their drinking of which I remind you, as you ought to be careful in your advocacy of temperance principles in a people so greatly addicted to alcohol'.

Despite these disadvantages – a newspaper commented disapprovingly on his 'blue ribbon and red neck-tie principles' – Murray was a great success in Glasgow. The chief interest of his time there, in the present context, rests in the glimpses he gives of the University then, as seen by a sensitive and imaginative outsider, who took nothing for granted. He was surprised to find that his first duty was to collect a part of his salary direct from the students who enrolled in his class: 'one took three guineas from student by student for about three days,' he recalled later, 'put the money each day into a stout leather bag and then, armed with a good walking stick, carried it to the bank. I was once advised to have a companion with a real cudgel, but cannot remember whether I did so.'

He was dismayed to find how much of his time the first few days was occupied in ensuring discipline in his class: 'It seems that the whole work is policing. You have, so I'm told, never to look at your book ... you keep your eyes wandering up and down every corner of the room, watching for insubordination ...' However, he soon asserted his authority, and was able to report that the students 'were very good and quiet except when, after I had described the process of consulting the Delphic Oracle, they were so pleased that they all applauded ... it seemed very strange.'

Most of his students were working for a general or pass degree, and Greek was still a compulsory subject. They expected to get their education from their lectures, not from private reading, and, since they were conscious of having paid their Professor directly, they demanded a high standard from him. His dismay soon gave way to admiration. He told his wife that he found a zeal for education which was absent at Oxford: 'A good many of

9 Buchanan Street in 1926

10 The Cunarder, *Queen Mary*, under construction at Clydebank (1934)

11a *Above:* The Willow Tea Room, Sauchiehall Street, designed by Charles Rennie Mackintosh

11b *Below:* The 1938 Empire Exhibition in Bellahouston Park

13 *Above:* A Partick 'steamie', 1955

12a *Opposite top:* Bomb damage to tenement houses on Clydeside, 1941

12b *Opposite below:* 'Queen Street Station' by Sir Muirhead Bone (1876-1953)

14a *Above:* The 1989 Cup Final at Hampden Park in which Celtic defeated Rangers 1-0

14b *Below:* The assorted domes and cupolas of the City Chambers are seen in the centre of this photograph, with the spire of Hutcheson's Hall in the foreground.

15 Argyle Steet and Anderston Cross, 1989

16 The Necropolis in winter.

them were older than I am. One gave an address seven miles from Glasgow, so Murdoch [his assistant] said, "I suppose ye'll come by train," to which he replied: "No, mon, I walk." He had to be with me by 8 a.m. Murdoch knew one man who used to walk twelve miles before the senior class; but he died in the first session. I suppose he had not enough to eat.' This was a long way from the privileged existence of most undergraduates at Oxford and Cambridge.

There was another difference: though women were not yet allowed to take degrees, he managed to introduce female undergraduates to his lectures; 'the men applauded when they came in'. Murray was something of an innocent and it does not seem to have occurred to him that the applause may have been ironical. Nevertheless he regarded these first steps in the provision of university education for women as 'the fulfilment of a cherished dream'. Murray believed in the emancipation of women; he saw that where there was economic oppression 'the weakest of the weak are women'; and he was able to do more in this respect in Glasgow than he would have been able to achieve in a less democratic university.

There was an élite in Glasgow, as in all universities, but because public lecturing was still the most important element in education there, professors were obliged to address themselves fully to the ordinary student. One of Murray's students was A.L. Lindsay, later the first Principal of Keele University. Looking back on his days at Glasgow, he said:

When I was a student, professors gave their best to the ordinary classes. The wonderful impression which A.C. Bradley and Gilbert Murray made on the students of the University was made through their ordinary classes, not on a mere handful of people who took honours in English or in Greek. That tradition ... produced in me the impression that anyone could teach honours subjects but that it required one's whole imagination and energy to teach the ordinary class.

The point about this emphasis on the wide diffusion of education was made by another of his students, Norman Leys, who later became a medical officer and critic of the colonial administration in East Africa, who, having commented that some 'professors feed passmen on the husks of scholarship and keep the interpretation of thought to a few whose minds are supposed to be able to support high ideas,' asked whether there was 'a greater need in the country than to give us ordinary men some clear vision of the main issues of life and some instruction on the way to use our minds on them?'

One of Murray's students was John Buchan, who first attracted his

73

Professor's attention when he approached him after a lecture to ask from what source Francis Bacon could have quoted a Latin translation of the Greek philosopher Democritus; this was a necessary rather than pretentious question, since the seventeen-year-old Buchan was engaged in editing a collection of Bacon's essays for a London publisher. In his autobiography, *Memory-Hold-The-Door* (1940), Buchan observed that Murray's lectures 'were, in Wordsworth's phrase, like "kindlings of the morning"'. They had that effect on many.

Buchan was not a typical undergraduate, and he was neither quite an outsider nor a Glaswegian. He had been born in Perth, and then spent the happiest parts of his boyhood among the Border hills of his beloved Tweedsmuir, but his father served as a Free Church Minister in the Gorbals, where Buchan himself taught Sunday School and learned something of the conditions of the slums, growing to admire the vitality of the children and deplore what life might make of them. Of his boyhood he oddly, or snobbishly, wrote: 'I never went to school in the conventional sense, for a boarding school was beyond the narrow means of my family,' but he attended 'an ancient grammar school on the south side of the river' [Hutcheson's] from which, at the age of seventeen, I passed to Glasgow University'. From there he would go on to Oxford, and then to the Bar in London to become in time an imperialist man of affairs in South Africa and Canada who lived in Scotland only on holiday and in his imagination.

He found that the University of Glasgow 'still smacked of the Middle Ages. The undergraduates lived in lodgings in the city and most of them cultivated the Muses on a slender allowance of oatmeal.' This was a romantic and inaccurate view: many were, after all, the sons of the prospering Glasgow bourgeoisie, and their diet was considerably more varied, as their means were greater. When Walter Elliot, the son of an auctioneer, became an undergraduate in 1905, his father provided him with a ground-floor flat in Blytheswood Drive, where he had five rooms, a housekeeper and Chippendale furniture inherited from an uncle. Elliot himself was not a typical undergraduate, but in a university with only two rules ('No dogs are admitted'; 'the gates close at 8 p.m.'), where there were no entrance exams, where you could remain an undergraduate as long as you paid your fees and were not convicted on a criminal charge, and where one man remained an undergraduate from the last year of Queen Victoria's reign to the first of George V's, there were probably as many undergraduates who lived in a manner approaching Elliot's as who subsisted on oatmeal.

When he came to write his autobiography in the last year of his life,

Buchan was infused with romantic nostalgia. He recalled that he would walk the four miles from the Gorbals to Gilmorehill to his eight o'clock class 'through every variety of the winter weather with which Glasgow fortifies her children'. Though much of his route was 'as ugly as anything you can find in Scotland' – an exaggeration, but he knew little of industrial Scotland beyond Glasgow – he found in memory that:

It was all a changing panorama of romance. There was the weather – fog like soup, drenching rains, winds that swirled down the cavernous streets, mornings that dawned bright and clear over snow. There was the sight of humanity going to work and the signs of awakening industry. There was the bridge with the river starred with strange lights, the lit shipping at the Broomielaw, and odours which even at their worst spoke of the sea. And at the end there were the gaunt walls of the college often seen in the glow of a West Highland sunrise.

In that last sentence at least, Buchan caught something of the surprising magic of Glasgow: that it is a Highland or Celtic city, crouching incongruously on the edge of the Lowlands.

He was, by his own account, 'wholly obscure' as an undergraduate. Unlike the generation of Walter Elliot and O. H. Mavor ('James Bridie'), he made no mark on the University, and left no legend there, despite his precocious publishing activity. This was fair enough: the University of Glasgow never conquered his heart as Oxford did. When he left Glasgow he scarcely returned except to visit his parents.

And yet Glasgow continued to exist, even to flourish, in his imagination. It plays a significant part in two of his novels. The first is *Mr Standfast*. This book, written while Buchan was Director of Propaganda during the First World War, takes Richard Hannay to Glasgow. He is working as an undercover agent, and one of his tasks is to investigate the degree of disenchantment with the war effort among the Glasgow working class. It was the time of the rent strikes and of trouble in the munition factories, of unrest in Ireland which – the authorities feared – might well spread to Glasgow; it was the time out of which the myth of Red Clydeside would grow. Buchan was concerned to allay the fears of those who should have known better than to entertain them. His picture of the Glasgow working man is respectful and temperate.

He returned to Glasgow in *Huntingtower* (1922). This novel is notable for its picture of the Gorbals Die-Hards, the slum children who had their origins in the Sunday School class of his father's kirk, 'used a' their days wi' sleepin' in coal rees and dunnies and dodgin' the polis'. Their leader is

Dougal, 'a stunted boy, who from his face might have been fifteen, but had the stature of a child of twelve'. His voice 'had a touch of Irish in it, a spice of music-hall patter, as well as the odd lilt of the Glasgow vernacular. He was strong in vowels, but the consonants, especially the letter "t", were only aspirations.' Another of the gang is introduced as 'Peer Pairson, a contraction presumably for Peter Paterson'. They are tough, amoral and resourceful. 'Do you breed many like that in Glasgow?' asks the English poet, John Heritage. 'Plenty,' is the reply.

Buchan has affectionate fun with the Gorbals Die-Hards, and, though sentimentalised, they are authentic enough. But this true tribute to Glasgow comes in the unlikely shape of the novel's hero, the retired grocer Dickson McCunn.

The novel begins just after Dickson McCunn has sold his grocer's shop in Mearns Street, 'together with the branches in Crossmyloof and the Shaws,' to a company called the United Supply Stores Ltd. Buchan throws this information off casually, but it is not without its social significance; it marks a moment when the West of Scotland bourgeoisie are moving from the status of proprietors to that of managers, when the independent retail businesses are giving way to chain stores. But Dickson's worth is recognised. When he goes to the bank, even in ancient tweeds,

> the chief cashier received him with deference in spite of his unorthodox garb, for he was not the least honoured of the bank's customers. As it chanced he had been talking about him that very morning to a gentleman from London. 'The strength of this city', he had said, tapping his eyeglasses on his knuckles, 'does not rest in its dozen very rich men, but in the hundred or two homely folk who make no parade of wealth. Men like Dickson McCunn, for example, who live all their life in a semi-detached villa and die worth half-a-million.

McCunn himself is a splendidly engaging figure, but he is rooted in reality. He is or has been an elder of the Guthrie Memorial Kirk, which is, presumably, the Free Kirk rather than the Church of Scotland. He is President of his kirk's Literary Society, and has been three times Chairman at Burns Anniversary Dinners. He has delivered 'Orations in eulogy of the national Bard; not because he greatly admired Burns – he thought him rather vulgar – but because he took Burns as an emblem of the un-Burns-like literature that he loved.'

Dickson McCunn is a romantic, perhaps an improbable one; his wife scarcely enters the story, but a brief sketch gives a vivid and accurate picture of a certain stratum of the Glasgow bourgeoisie. When Dickson embarks on the walking-holiday which will make his dreams of adventure unpleasant and alarming reality, Mrs McCunn is herself on holiday at the Neuk Hydropathic. This is her 'earthly paradise ... where she put on her afternoon dress and every jewel she possessed when she rose in the morning, ate large meals of which the novelty atoned for the nastiness, and collected an immense causal acquaintance with whom she discussed ailments, ministers, sudden deaths, and the intricate genealogies of her class.' 'Mamma's enjoying herself fine,' Mr McCunn informs the tea-pot. For his own part he hates hydropathics, detesting the food and the Turkish baths, having, unlike the upper or lower classes, 'a passionate aversion to bearing his body before strangers'. He therefore avoids them, but has been accustomed to spend his holiday month 'decorously with his wife in some seaside villa'.

Buchan indulges in some gentle fun at McCunn's expense, but his portrait is as affectionate as it is accurate; and in one scene he allows Dickson to express the author's understanding of the importance of the middle classes. John Heritage, with whom he has fallen into conversation in an inn, has told him 'I've no use for the upper classes and the middle classes. There's only one class that matters, the plain man, the workers, who live close to life ...,' and has reproached him for idealising tinkers and gypsies. Dickson admits the charge: 'But you're at the same job yourself.' He tells Heritage that he himself has come out of the working class and lived next to them all his life:

> You idealise the working man, you and your kind, because you're ignorant. You say that he's seeking for truth, when he's only looking for a drink and a rise in wages. You tell me that he's near reality, but I tell you that his notion of reality is often just a short working-day and looking on at a footba'-match on Saturday .... And when you run down the middle classes that do three-quarters of the world's work and keep the machine going and the working man in a job, then I tell you you're talking havers. Havers!

His defence of the bourgeoisie is endorsed from another quarter. When their adventures are over, the Russian Princess Saskia tells her fiancé, a Russian nobleman who has become an engineer in Australia, that she does not understand Dickson:

> he is the *petit bourgeois*, the *épicier*, the class which the world ridicules .... The others with good fortune I might find elsewhere – in Russia perhaps. But not Dickson. 'No,' is the answer. You will not find him in Russia. He is what they call the middle-class, which we who are foolish used to laugh at. But he is the stuff which above all others makes a great people. He will endure when

aristocracies crack and proletariats crumble. In our own land we have never known him, but till we create him our land will not be a nation.

These words represent Buchan's recognition of what the middle classes have meant to Glasgow and to Scotland.

Edwin Muir's experience of the city was quite different from Murray's or Buchan's. Murray floated over it, Buchan rose out of it, Muir tumbled headlong into it. He was transported from an idyllic childhood in Orkney to a Glasgow tenement where you had to lock the door and to learn never to admit the beggars who were 'perpetually ringing the bell'. He worked first as a clerk in an office, and had to walk there from his home on the south side through slums, which he was unable to invest with the qualities that the more fortunate Buchan found among their inhabitants. On the contrary, his daily journeys filled him 'with a deep sense of degradation: the crumbling houses, the twisted faces, the obscene words heard casually in passing, the ancient, haunting stench of pollution and decay, the arrogant women, the mean men, the terrible children, frightened me, and at last filled me with an immense, blind dejection.' Eventually he grew accustomed, and 'walked through the slums as if they were an ordinary road leading from my home to my work ...' Even so, he retained the feeling, 'passing through Eglinton Street or Crown Street, that I was dangerously close to the ground, deep down in a place from which I might never be able to climb up again'. It was a similar awareness which fostered the cult of respectability among the skilled workers and lower middle class of any industrial city, a consciousness of how thin was the ice through which they might fall into the abyss of the slums. Muir thought of them as 'a great, spreading swamp into which I might sink for ever'.

For many, such fears were primarily economic. Unemployment, illness, improvidence or misfortune – any of these might remove the safety net that protected a man from degradation. For Muir the fear was moral: that he might come to accept that this was the way things had to be, that this was the ultimate truth about life. When he escaped he was horrified to think that for the great majority the story ends as it began, and 'their lives remain to their death a waste of rubbish, second-rate and second-hand, raked from the great dustheap .... The thought that life can be for tens of thousands what it was to me after I came to Glasgow – and far worse, for I have never lived in a slum – painfully troubles me; for it means that human life can be made up of rubbish streaked with all the great major catastrophes of human life, like a pudding made of cheap ingredients, except for the tragedy, which is real.'

Muir's reflections on Glasgow are to be found in his *Autobiography* (1954), and his *Scottish Journey* (1935). The first refers back to the first decade of the century while the second is set in the middle of the 1930s, but what he saw then was informed by what he had experienced earlier. The principal difference was that the economic system which he found reprehensible, had been apparently flourishing while he was a youth, and seemed to have crumbled by the time of his adult return. Indeed he ends his account of Glasgow in *Scottish Journey* by observing that 'the fundamental realities of Glasgow are economic' and asking 'how is this collapsing city to be put on its feet again?'

What he has to say about Glasgow is of unusual interest because Muir was, on account of his quivering sensibility and the nature of his intellect, quite untypical. He had a penetrating mind, which could simultaneously illuminate and distort what he saw. It was a mind that always sought for significance, and so sometimes found significance in what others accepted uncritically or unquestioningly. So he found at first that the people of Glasgow seemed to him like 'sad and incomprehensible distortions of nature'. They contradicted everything that he had been brought up to believe. They were the products of 'a system which forces them to gather money out of the dirt'. But the self-protective need to ignore this involves a deliberate blunting of one whole area of their sensibility. Muir was appalled by the people 'whose main ideal was respectability or rising in the world'. (He didn't ask what they would have been if they had not had this ideal.) Yet he saw why they did it: it was 'because of the intense squalor of the surroundings amid which the go-getter lived'.

He pointed out that 'the slums not only penetrate the lives of all classes in Glasgow, affecting their ideas and their most personal emotions . . . but also send out a dirty wash into the neatest and remotest suburbs, and even the surrounding countryside, so that it is possible for one to feel that the whole soil for miles around is polluted'. They spread contagion, but this was moral as well as physical and the moral element was more important. In his view it was the awareness of the slums which provoked, and justified, the Calvinist cult of success. 'Inherited Calvinism was at the bottom of their [the respectably minded] contemptuous reprobation of anyone, who, out of weakness or amiability or scruple, refrained from striving to his utmost to make money; for their attitude to such people was indistinguishable from that of the elect to the damned a century before.' This was allied to 'an orthodox economic theory which taught that competition was equally necessary to increase the general wealth and strengthen the individual character'.

Such views were held all over those parts of Western Europe and the

American Continent which had prospered as a result of Industrialism and the expansion of commerce. Muir perhaps only found them in surpassing degree in Glasgow because that was the city he knew in his impressionable youth. Yet they were certainly there; they were characteristically Glaswegian and characteristically Scottish, whether he was justified in attributing them to an inherited Calvinism or not. When he returned to Glasgow in the 1930s, their validity seemed disproved by the Depression. There were many in Glasgow at that time who would never be persuaded to believe in that 'orthodox economic theory' again. In our own time indeed its recrudescence in England has been widely condemned as contrary to a Scottish tradition, an opinion which would have surprised Muir, who saw it as an essential element in Glasgow's character. He believed that its consequences could be as damaging for the rich who benefited from the theory as for the poor whom he classed as its victims: 'the rich have psychologically a far greater burden to bear than the poor; ostentation is one of the most obvious means of blinding themselves to it; and in this way perhaps the lives of the Glasgow rich can be explained ...'

Muir's analysis of Glasgow is penetrating and deserves to be read in full. It is, I think, valid; yet it never contrives to get beyond analysis. Ultimately his ability to dissect the nature of industrial society, with Glasgow as the body stretched on the table of his anatomical laboratory, failed to suggest a means whereby the advantages of Industrialism could be preserved without the concomitant hardships. In his youth he inclined towards Socialism, finding virtue in those trade unionists who 'saw before them the life of a workman: that is, a life which could never escape into riches or even into moderate comfort. They embraced that life without a thought of rising from it except with all their fellow-workmen. If such devotion or fidelity are not to be admired, then all our ideas of morality are mistaken.' Later he lost faith in Socialism on account of the element of compulsion. Yet in his highlighting of the conflict between individual and communal values which he discerned in Glasgow, he pointed to a continuing argument. Nineteenth-century Glasgow was an individualistic city; twentieth-century Glasgow has emphasised communal values. Will the next century be able to effect a synthesis?

Half a century later another outsider, a man of an originality and sensibility akin to Muir's, wrote about Glasgow. This was R.F. Mackenzie, schoolmaster, sage, iconoclast and perpetual questioner of conventional wisdom. He remarked, scathingly, 'economic forces (we are told) created the Glasgow desert – the grey highrise flats, the lower tenements of red and brown brick, the streets of blackened sandstone, an abandon of weeds in open spaces ... it's an ungainly builder's yard.' What hope have we, he asked, 'of mitigating the savagery of greed'? It seemed to him, coming from country districts, that 'something ruthless and non-human has taken over, implacable, inexorable'. Even the University failed to ask the questions it should ask. Glasgow, he wrote, 'is the product of a society that doesn't know where it is going, whose God has led it up a blind alley ....'

Critics such as Mackenzie and Muir are necessary. One can reply that no society knows where it is going, that Glasgow made itself in ignorance, that society as such is incapable of self-knowledge, even of any knowledge, this being the property of individuals. The objections could be multiplied, all valid; their validity would not, however, render the criticisms invalid. A city such as Glasgow confronts one with imponderables, which yet require to be weighed, with questions too profound for single answers about the nature of the way we live, and of the forms of life which we have inherited. One can balance Buchan's Dickson McCunn against the 'depraved knowledge' which Muir found in people's faces; one can confront the Gorbals Die-Hards and their chief's confident assertion that 'ye'll no fickle Tammas Yownie' with Muir's statement that 'the sufferings of an ordinary healthy child brought up in the slums are dreadful beyond imagination. The terror and corrupt knowledge of these children can be heard in their voices, the most desolate and discordant sound in creation.' One can contrast Murray's faith in the enduring value of scholarship and his admiration for the dedication of his poor students with Mackenzie's conviction that 'what they communicate [at the University] is their master's voice'.

Economic forces made Glasgow; but economic forces do not exist independent of human will. Economic theories land us in moral quagmires, because man is not only an economic being. Solzhenitsyn recognises the paradox: 'Freedom of action and prosperity are necessary if man is to stand up straight on this earth, but spiritual greatness dwells in eternal subordination, in awareness of yourself as an insignificant particle.' Glasgow was made by men who believed utterly in self-fulfilment, and the world they created denied the possibility of this to countless others. In one way or another, all the outsiders of this chapter brooded and struggled with that dilemma: how do you make an industrial city serve its inhabitants? By what means do you prevent service from becoming slavery? Is Glasgow better expressed by the Art Gallery in Kelvingrove or by Barlinnie Jail? The two examples are not chosen at random, or for rhetorical effect. A connection exists: both are products of the industrial system: the art gallery which elevates and delights; the prison which confines and debases.

CHAPTER EIGHT

HOW RED WAS CLYDESIDE?

In the General Election of 1923 the ILP (Independent Labour Party) won ten of Glasgow's fifteen constituencies. It was an unprecedented triumph. Exultant crowds saw the new Members of Parliament off from St Enoch's station. They sang 'The Red Flag' and two Psalms, the 23rd and 124th – 'had not the Lord been on our side/When cruel men/Against us furiously/Rose up in wrath/To make of us their prey'. One of the new MPs, either James Maxton or David Kirkwood – accounts vary – called out, 'Don't hurry for the train – it'll all belong to the People when we come back.'

The scene was, as it turned out, the high-water mark of revolutionary Glasgow; indeed the Clydesiders promised a revolution that ebbed away. Maxton assured the crowds at the station that they 'would see the atmosphere of the Clyde getting the better of the House of Commons'; the reverse happened.

Yet, fifteen years earlier, any suggestion that revolutionary ideas would get even so far would have been dismissed derisively in Glasgow. The city contained many Socialist preachers, but it had proved barren ground for Socialism. In 1892 only a quarter of shipyard workers had been trade union members. Beatrice Webb, visiting Glasgow five years later, observed ruefully that 'the Scottish nature does not lend itself to combination'. The tradition among the skilled working class was one of self-help and self-improvement. A man who had mastered a trade was his own master, whoever he worked for. The contempt with which the Irish under-class was regarded had also contributed to the slow unionisation of the city's workers.

The first, or at least first grave, challenge to the complacency inherent in this attitude was offered by the unemployment crisis of 1907–8. *The Times* reported that 16,000 people in Govan were 'on the verge of starvation'. A demonstration drew 35,000 to Glasgow Green. But this depression was short-lived, for the naval rearmament programme helped to provide work for the unused capacity of yards such as John Brown's, Fairfield's and Beardmore's. Socialists preached the brotherhood of man and universal peace, but warships, revolving gun turrets and munitions were good for Glasgow, however artificial a market they might represent. If, on the whole, employers in Glasgow had little sympathy for unions, their skilled workforce were hardly more enthusiastic. Harry McShane, of the British Socialist Party – one of many small groups – recalled that 'it wasn't easy to rouse up the engineers; they were very respectable with their blue suits and bowler hats and used to come to mass meetings with umbrellas.'

Nevertheless even before the war there was a plethora of Socialist groups in Glasgow. There were Socialist Sunday Schools – Buchan's Wee Jaikie of the Gorbals Die-Hards attended one and learned songs such as 'Class-conscious are we and class-conscious wull be/Till our fit's on the neck of the Boorjoyzee', though he joined because he heard they were 'for fechtin' battles' and left when he discovered 'there was no magic lantern or swaree at Christmas'. There was the Glasgow branch of William Morris's Socialist League and the Clarion Scouts, whom Edwin Muir joined. They held lectures in the Metropole Theatre every Sunday evening, and Muir could remember Ramsay MacDonald 'speaking with great passion and saying nothing for two hours' and Edward Carpenter taking the audience into his confidence and telling them how he had his clothes made without any lining so that he could wash them himself: 'He seemed to expect his working-class audience to follow his example.' The ILP, the SDF (Social Democratic Federation), the Syndicalists, the Anarchists and many other motley and short-lived groupings all held their animated and inconclusive meetings. If, however, nothing was concluded, or scarcely begun, a ferment of left-wing argumentativeness gradually influenced the young. More serious was the Workers' Educational Association, and more enduring the influence of John Maclean, the hero or Bonnie Prince Charlie of Scottish Socialism, the Herald of the Revolution that never came.

Maclean was born in Glasgow in 1879, and lived all his life there, but, like so many Glaswegians, he belonged to the broken and dispossessed peasantry of the Highlands. He was the heir of a culture thrust by economic circumstances into the industrial city. His father died when the boy was nine. His mother, a McPhee, worked as a weaver, then kept a shop, then took in lodgers. Maclean wrote that 'it was the sacrifices she made ... to enable me to be educated which made me resolve to use my education in the service of the workers'. Bred in the nineteenth-century Scottish tradition of self-help, he was persuaded by the evidence of the hardship he saw around him that it was inadequate.

He trained as a teacher in Glasgow's Free Church College, and graduated in Political Economy at the University. He was a founder member of the Glasgow Teachers' Socialist Society, and, though he abandoned the Christianity of the Original Secession Church in which he had been reared, his Socialism, like that of so many of his generation, was always coloured by the influence of the Protestant culture in which he had been formed: in 1918 he told the Durham miners that 'the mantle of Jesus Christ has fallen on the Bolsheviks'.

Before 1914 Maclean was known as a lecturer and organiser of the unemployed and unskilled workers. He had joined the SDF, the most Marxist of the many Socialist groups, which was founded by the eccentric Old Etonian H.M. Hyndman. He taught in a Govan school and his public lectures on Sunday afternoons attracted audiences of as many as a thousand. It was the First World War, however, which made him a figure of more than local importance. He opposed it from the start. In his view, it was merely the outcome of the struggle for markets between the capitalist powers. As a logical theoretician he might have welcomed it as a necessary stage in the disintegration of capitalism, but he was revolted by the idea that workers should be killed to make capitalists richer, and within a couple of years was calling for 'a Socialist revolution'. Not surprisingly, he was dismissed by the Govan School Board after he had been charged with 'using language likely to cause a breach of the peace', and in a few months was again arrested and charged under the Defence of the Realm Act with having tried to discourage recruitment and having impeded the production of war materials. He was sentenced to three years' penal servitude. The *Scotsman* described him as 'a representative of a poisonous set of parasites who talk treason instead of working'. He was released fifteen months later partly as a result of huge demonstrations in Glasgow, partly on account of the Government's desire to appease unrest.

Maclean himself, however, was not appeased. The Bolshevik coup against Kerensky's revolutionary government in Russia delighted him. The Bolsheviks in turn named him an honorary president of the First Congress of Soviets and as their consul in Scotland. The Government, which refused to recognise the Bolshevik Government, declined to accept its consul.

In March 1918 he was arrested again and charged with sedition. He refused to plead and instead told the court, 'I am here as the accuser of Capitalism dripping with blood from head to foot.' He got five years. The sentence aroused fury in Glasgow, or at least among Labour supporters there. The Clyde District Defence Committee demanded his release. The Gorbals Labour Party chose him as their Parliamentary candidate, even though there was already a Labour MP. He went on hunger strike and was subjected to the vile practice of forcible feeding. When he was released in December 1918, his health was broken.

His views became wilder. As the Labour movement advanced to the centre of politics, Maclean became irrelevant to its progress. He called for the establishment of a Workers' Republic of Scotland: 'Glasgow could be made a Petrograd, a Revolutionary centre second to none.' Any appeal such a demand might have had was vitiated by the incoherent rhetoric with which it was surrounded. Maclean prophesied a war between Britain and the USA for control of the Pacific, and claimed that only the establishment of a Workers' Republic of Scotland could save the country from such involvement.

Wild talk like this, and vague stuff about 'the Communism of the clans', discredited Maclean, with Willie Gallacher, the future Communist Member of Parliament, even concluding that Maclean was now mentally unbalanced. He may have been; certainly his grasp of reality and sense of the possible were diminished. He was still loved, but had lost political credibility. He was well beaten in the contest for the Gorbals seat in the General Election of 1923, and died later that year, of pneumonia caught while still campaigning in Gorbals.

Maclean has become the hero-martyr of the Scottish Left, especially in Glasgow. Hugh MacDiarmid called him 'one of the few true men in our sordid breed/A flash of sun in a country all prison-grey'; absurd but memorable lines. Hamish Henderson struck the line 'when Maclean comes to the Broomielaw' in his song 'Freedom, Come All Ye'. His career cannot be called a failure, for he lives in poetry and memory. Nevertheless he was ineffective compared with more flexible and pragmatic contemporaries in the Labour movement.

There were two strands to the creation of Glasgow as a Labour-dominated city. Both made it certain that, in reality, Glasgow would emerge as pink rather than red. The first was the development of organised Labour seeking limited practical advantages; the second the attraction of Roman Catholics to the Labour movement.

The war promoted the first. Despite the opposition to war of Labour Party Leaders in 1914, it was initially popular in Glasgow. 'Men rushed to join the army hoping the war wouldn't be all over by the time they got to the front,' recalled Harry McShane. The Corporation raised two battalions from its tramway employees; within twenty-four hours a thousand men had volunteered. The industries which produced war materials naturally kept, or tried to keep, their work-force; these were exempt when conscription was introduced in 1916. Except for a strike at Fairfield's in 1915, industrial peace prevailed in the shipyards. Things were different in the engineering works.

There were two reasons, which worked upon each other, as is usually the way in industrial disputes. First the employers, particularly William Weir of G. & J. Weir, were anxious to change some of the industry's working practices, which were old-fashioned in comparison to those of foreign competitors, and saw the war as offering an opportunity of doing so; in fairness to them, the greater demands made by the wartime economy rendered reform of working practices necessary. On the other hand, a group of shop stewards who formed themselves into the Clyde Workers Committee (CWC) recognised an opportunity also: they could use the exigencies of the war to promote their claim for at least a degree of workers' control. They were able to play on the fears of the skilled men that the policy of maximising production, demanded by the Ministry of Munitions, coupled with the reform of working practices which Weir and other employers sought, would result in what they called 'dilution'; that is the replacement of skilled workers by machines operated by at best a semi-skilled work-force which might even be composed of women. This fear was more acute because such dilution might cost them their exemption from military service.

These tensions and conflicting interests bred discontent and led to a series of incidents such as the 'tuppence an hour' strike of 1915, disputes over the Clearance Certificates demanded under the Munitions Act before a man could change his job, and over dilution. In 1916 Lloyd George, the Minister for Munitions, addressed a meeting which was disrupted by the CWC shop stewards and their supporters. The activists were deported to Edinburgh, but were freed the following summer, and the CWC was soon functioning again with the Communist Gallacher as its chairman. By then, however, a compromise had been effected; the unions were allowed to control details of dilution. Leaders such as David Kirkwood and Emmanuel Shinwell, the latter a future Labour Minister, now found themselves happy to co-operate with the Government and employers, because they had been granted a certain authority for policy and management.

Things changed in the last winter of the war. In January 1918 the Director of National Service, Sir Auckland Geddes, tried to persuade the Glasgow shop stewards that the need for men in the forces was now so great that conscription must be extended even to the exempted skilled workers; they responded by passing an anti-war resolution.

At the same time the Bolshevik coup encouraged Labour militancy. A huge demonstration was held in Glasgow on May day 1918, and solidarity with the Bolsheviks was widely approved. In January 1919 the CWC called a strike in support of a claim for a shorter working week, which they hoped might avert threatened post-war unemployment; this was itself, however, an indication that militancy had reached, or was at any rate approaching, its peak, for the threat of unemployment would make the work-force more defensive and therefore quiescent. But the CWC tried to convert their strike into a General Strike of all Glasgow workers, and this led to a riot when the police charged a body of demonstrators in George Square who were thought to be trying to disrupt the power supply for the tramcars. This persuaded the Secretary of State for Scotland, Robert Munro, to declare in Cabinet 'that it was more clear than ever that it was a misnomer to call the situation in Glasgow a strike – it was a Bolshevist rising'. This was nonsense, though understandable; the strike leaders, such as Shinwell and Kirkwood, had no thought of anything beyond industrial protest, but memories of the Russian revolution made the Cabinet panic. On 1 February, Glasgow woke to find half a dozen tanks in the Cattle Market, a howitzer at the City Chambers and machine-gunners manning the Post Office. Kirkwood, Shinwell and Gallacher were arrested, and the strike soon petered out.

The exaggerated response contributed to the creation of the myth of Red Clydeside. A few months later the last of the Labour members of the Lloyd George Coalition, George Barnes, MP for Gorbals, left the Cabinet; Glasgow, it seemed, had ranged itself against the political establishment. It had lost the first battle, but the war could yet be won. It was in this mood that after the 1922 election triumph, the Clydesiders advanced on Westminster. They would make little real impression there, soon succumbing to its soothing atmosphere. 'Like a cobra, the Commons slowly swallowed and digested the combative Clydesiders and so did Transport House. It is hard luck to be swallowed by two cobras,' was the judgement passed by the Glasgow journalist Colm Brogan in 1952. Nevertheless the organisation achieved by the working-class movement during the First World War, and the tradition of militant solidarity then created, contributed to the conversion of the Glasgow working class from Liberalism to Labour, and to the eventual establishment of Labour as the dominant force in local politics.

The other element in this process was the adhesion of the city's Irish Catholic community to Labour. Traditionally they had voted Liberal, for the Liberals were the party which supported Home Rule for Ireland. They were deterred from supporting Labour, partly because the Trade Union movement was still largely the preserve of the groups of skilled workers, among whom Catholics were still few, and who were largely hostile to them. 'No Irish Here' was a notice frequently attached to engineering shops.

A still more important deterrent was the Church's hostility to Socialism, which it linked with atheism. The clergy held by Leo XIII's 1878 encyclical *Quod Apostolici muneris* had condemned 'that class of men who, under various and strange names, are known as Socialists, Communists or Nihilists ...'

By 1922 all this had changed. The Catholic population of Glasgow had been alienated from the Liberal Party by the harsh suppression of the 1916 Easter Rising in Dublin, and then by Lloyd George's policy of counter-terrorism in Ireland marked by his use of the Black-and-Tan irregular forces. No party which pursued such a policy could hope to retain the support of those who were compatriots and co-religionists of its victims.

Second, the priests had abated their opposition to Socialism, partly because they feared its attraction for young men, and decided individually, rather than collectively, that the best means of averting Socialist revolution was to take charge of the potentially revolutionary movement, and partly because there had developed a strain of distinctively Catholic Socialism.

Its most important representative was John Wheatley. He was himself an immigrant, born in County Waterford, but he was brought up in Scotland, his father having found work in the Lanarkshire mines. Though his own early political interests were directed to Ireland as a member of the United Irish League, he was to do more than any other individual to spain the Irish in the West of Scotland from that cause, and to make Glasgow a Labour city.

Wheatley was a man of rare intellectual and practical ability. In 1906 he founded the Catholic Socialist Society, and in the same year set up in business as a printer and publisher. He launched two publications: the *Catholic Working Man* and the *Catholic Socialist*; eventually he would be a newspaper proprietor, his most successful paper the *Glasgow Evening Standard*. His business success distinguished him from his Parliamentary colleagues (he was elected for Shettleston in the 1922 ILP triumph); he was able to send his children to a Catholic fee-paying school and live in a solidly bourgeois house overlooking a golf course. When he died in 1930 he left £16,000. His success, however, did not lure him to the right politically. He declared that his Socialism emanated 'from that spirit of brotherhood which is ever present in the hearts of men but which is often suppressed by the struggle for existence'. This faith has been, however corrupted at times, a distinguishing feature of the Glasgow Labour Party. It was a long way from Marx, but owed much to Leo XIII's later encyclical *Rerum Novarum* which attacked capitalism from a Catholic viewpoint. That was always Wheatley's position. When he became disillusioned with the Labour Party in the last years of his life, he told Beatrice Webb that 'he would be a Communist if he was not a pious Catholic'. Sir Oswald Mosley judged that he was 'the only man of Lenin's quality the English [sic] Left ever produced'. He was saved from any temptation to try to emulate Lenin by his Catholicism, and he provided the essential bridge by which Catholics could cross over into the Labour Party.

He was elected to the Glasgow Corporation in 1923. His main interest lay then in housing policy. Despite the slum clearance schemes of the last thirty years, this was – as Edwin Muir's testimony had indicated – a disgrace to humanity. Wheatley advocated using the profits from Glasgow's successful municipal enterprises to subsidise the building of cottages. His pamphlet, *Eight-Pound Cottages for Glasgow Citizens* (1918) began thus: 'Dr Chalmers, Chief Medical Officer of Health for Glasgow, has just issued his report for last year. Commenting on it the *Glasgow Herald* remarks that it "reflects a year of normal experience". In this case the normal is horrible.' T.C. Smout has observed that 'this understanding that "the normal is horrible" in working class experience, and the faith that something could be done by the working-class to change it, was the key to the appeal of Wheatley's party'. Importantly, it was a key to which no priest could object; the transformation of Socialism into social work, which has been a characteristic of Glasgow Labour, satisfied the Catholic Church, and bound working-class Catholics firmly to the Labour Party.

Wheatley's achievement should not be minimised. On the Continent Socialist parties were violently anti-clerical; in Italy the young Socialist Mussolini was denouncing the priests as 'black microbes', servants of capitalism, persecutors of Jews, and poisoners of young minds'. The use of such language in Glasgow would have kept Labour a marginal, or at least minority, party. The Labour movement was fortunate to have a man such as Wheatley capable of eschewing such nonsense and drawing decent working-class Catholics into its fold.

The direction Glasgow Labour would take was determined by Wheatley's activity as Minister of Health in the first Labour Government of 1923. He was regarded as the only successful minister and his Housing (Financial Provisions) Act as the administration's only legislative achievement. It provided for central government funding of local authorities which undertook the building of houses to approved standards but stipulated that these houses should be built for rent only and not for sale. Unfortunately the result was far from the attractive cottages that Wheatley himself had called for. The bleak housing estates, many of which were to degenerate into slums within thirty years of being built, were distantly derived from the garden suburbs proposed by Ebenezer Howard in England; but the distance was more marked than the derivation. Nevertheless the homes they provided were welcome at the time. This extension of municipal Socialism, a logical development of the municipalisation policies of the old Glasgow Corporation, made Town Councils landlords on a scale, and with a power over their tenants, such as no private landlord could have dreamed of. It was Wheatley's major achievement. The policies of the Glasgow Corporation, of which Labour won control in 1933, represented a victory for Socialism conceived as an ameliorating, rather than revolutionary, force.

One other measure bound the Catholic community to Labour. This was the Education Act of 1918, which, ironically, was brought in by the Liberal Secretary of State in the Coalition Ministry, Robert Munro. Among other provisions it granted state finance to Catholic schools. Voluntary Catholic schools had existed since 1872. They were inadequately financed and therefore starved of resources. Munro described them as being 'generally speaking, inferior as regards housing and equipment, their teachers zealous but poorly paid, their provision of secondary schools totally inadequate and the educational outlook of the mass of their children unduly narrowing'. His Act provided support, while enabling them to retain their autonomy; it facilitated the emergence of a Catholic middle class. The Government's Irish policy cost them any gratitude they might have expected from this enlightened policy, and it was Labour who proved the beneficiaries. While the Protestant-dominated Moderates on Glasgow Corporation denounced the scheme as offering 'Rome on the rates', Labour prudently backed it. The alliance between the Catholic Church and the Labour Party in the West of Scotland was accordingly cemented.

CHAPTER NINE

CITY OF CELTS

'There is no subject on which writers and speakers about Glasgow are less willing to dwell than that of the Irish in Scotland,' wrote C. M. Oakley, author of 'The Second City' (1967). This was probably true, with the odd consequence that, as Tom Gallagher has put it in a valuable article 'Catholics in Scottish Politics' (*Bulletin of Scottish Politics*, vol II, 1989) 'dispassionate comment about Scotland's largest minority group was so seldom forthcoming that well into the 20th century many people were unaware that the great majority of "Irish" were in fact Scottish-born. It was as early as the 1880s that the Catholic community taking root in mainly Protestant Scotland ceased to be directly Irish.' Nevertheless, as Moray McLaren, himself a Scottish Catholic, put it: 'For the ordinary douce or dour Lowland Scottish Glaswegian, their presence in the city did present a problem. No matter how ardently they proclaimed and felt themselves to be sons of Glasgow and Scotland, their religion and their habit of marrying amongst themselves seemed to separate them from the more purely indigenous descendants of the old Glasgow.' This separation was made still more visible after the passing of the 1918 Education Act ensured the survival of Catholic schools; it has been one of the principal tasks of the Labour Party to reconcile the two strains. This has been largely accomplished. Yet differences remain, evident in culture and awareness of history. One such was exemplified by the novelist William McIlvanney when he informed a Scottish National Party Conference in 1987 that the history of Wallace and Bruce, John Knox and Mary Queen of Scots, and the Jacobites was 'irrelevant'. Few people of purely Scottish extraction would agree with him.

It may be that the distrust of Glasgow which is still evident in other parts of Scotland, and which contributed to the defeat at Westminster of the 1979 Referendum on the scheme of political devolution proposed in the Scotland Act, owes something to the residual awareness of the difference of the Glasgow Irish, but it is more likely that the cause is the city's distinct identity, peculiar economic problems and demographic dominance. However that may be, the character of Glasgow has been formed to a considerable extent by Irish immigration, and by the descendants of those immigrants. They have helped to make the city which was once distinguished for its narrow Covenanting zeal the cosmopolitan and heterogenous place it is today.

Glasgow still has a reputation as a city disfigured by sectarianism which can lead to violence. This is particularly associated with football. Rangers and Celtic are the two best-known names in the city, even though an English reporter who telephoned me the other day said 'Keltic'. Both clubs owe their origins, and the passionate myths that encrust them, to Ireland; together they show how the Irish inheritance has become transformed into something perfectly Scottish. 'Rangers and Celtic were not football teams,' the novelist and journalist Cliff Hanley has written, 'they were banners under which Glaswegians could foam at the mouth.'

Celtic were the Catholic club, and Rangers the Protestant, Fenians on one side and the Orange Order on the other; and they remained like this even though Celtic were soon playing Protestants and indeed achieved their greatest triumph, the first British team to win the European Cup in 1967, under a Protestant manager, Jock Stein. Such displays of tolerance meant nothing because it was the support that continued to divide on the old sectarian basis. Once in the 1930s a Protestant playing for Celtic was howled at as 'a Fenian bastard'; a team-mate consoled him with the assurance that they called him that all the time, only to receive the reply, 'Aye, but you are a Fenian bastard.'

The rivalry was intense and unending. It led to a number of disgraceful scenes over the years. For example, the flames of bigotry flared up again in 1989 when Rangers recruited a talented former Celtic player. Yet their existence, and the passion directed at them, sublimated religious antagonism even while it was thought to fan it. It allowed for the generally innocent expenditure of angry emotion; it enabled the bile of bias and resentment, hatred and fear, to be spewed out without consequence. The divisions would have been as real even if Rangers and Celtic had never existed; perhaps it was necessary to invent them.

The railway viaduct over Argyle Street that leads into Central station is known as the 'Highlandman's Umbrella'; it is a reminder that the Celtic component of Glasgow's population is not restricted to those of Irish origin. Indeed, as the Glasgow telephone directory will confirm, Glasgow is a Highland city. More Gaelic is still spoken in Glasgow than in any city this side of the Atlantic. Indeed more Gaelic is spoken there than in the

Highlands and Islands themselves. As far back as the eighteenth century Bailie Nicol Jarvie confessed to Highland blood – 'my mother was a MacGregor – I carena wha kens it' – and the evictions and clearances of the eighteenth and nineteenth centuries saw large numbers of dispossessed Highlanders descend on Glasgow in search of sustenance and employment, if not fortune. In the latter part of the century many of these newcomers would congregate under the railway viaduct in Argyle Street on a Sunday afternoon, as a place where they could hope to meet friends from the same glen or island; which is why it became known as the 'Highlandman's Umbrella'.

Many of them lived a double life, not in a metaphorical or reprehensible sense, but actually and wisely. John M. Bannerman, rugby internationalist, farmer, broadcaster and Liberal politician, gives a vivid picture of it in his Memoirs (1972): 'My love of Glasgow and its people has, because of my upbringing, a deep Celtic root. I suggest that the roots transplanted from the soil of Gaeldom and set deep in the dark, crowded streets yielded sap that strengthened the Glasgow tree.'

Bannerman himself was born in Glasgow, in Shawlands on the south side, in 1901. His grandfather had come to the city from South Uist in 1873 as a result of a potato famine that coincided with a drought. The family's connection with Glasgow went further back, for John Bannerman's great-grandfather had settled there when he returned from the Battle of Waterloo 'with twelve grapeshot wounds in his body' to discover that his people had been evicted from their croft in the Strath of Kildonan. He married a MacDonald from South Uist who was on a visit to her uncle in Glasgow, and when he died his widow took their young son back to her own island.

Bannerman's father was seven when the family returned to Glasgow. He spoke only Gaelic, which was the language that continued to be spoken in their household for at least the next generation; it was John Bannerman's first language.

His father, John Roderick Bannerman, went to work for the Post Office as a telegraph boy when he was thirteen. It was employment such as many Highland mothers sought for their sons; it represented security which was naturally prized by those whose arrival in the city had been precipitated by deprivation of security. For this reason the Glasgow Police Force (and indeed the Metropolitan Police in London) contained a disproportionate number of Highlanders; Glasgow's hospitals were also chiefly staffed by Highland nurses and Highland ancillary workers. Bannerman attended night-classes at Glasgow High School and eventually rose to be a senior superintendent in the Glasgow GPO.

His son records that his father lived in two worlds: the Lowland one of work, 'bustle and competition' – though Government service such as the Post Office represented some degree of rejection of the competitive ethos characteristic of Glasgow – and the Gaelic world of home and friends. He was a founder of the *Ceilidh Nan Gaidheal*, the Highlanders' Ceilidh, which met every Saturday night in the West Regent Street Gael Lodge of the Freemasons. Up to three hundred people might attend to hear a lecture and participate in discussion; it was all in Gaelic, not a word of English being allowed. There was a rival group which held bilingual ceilidhs in the High School, much deplored by the traditionalists, but of value in perpetuating the language among members of families of Highland extraction who no longer used it habitually at home.

John Roderick Bannerman was an elder of St Columba Church, in St Vincent Street, where a Gaelic service was held at eleven o'clock every Sunday. It was through membership of the Church's Gaelic choir that he met his wife, a MacDonald from Skye. The younger Bannerman recalled that St Columba 'was a worldly church in the estimation of some, compared to, say, the Gaelic Free Presbyterian Church of St Jude's. Nevertheless, St Columba Church was the satisfying spiritual centre for succeeding generations of Highlanders, no matter how scattered their homes were in Glasgow.' On the way back from Sunday service talk would soon move from a dissection of the sermon to memories of their glens and islands. Though they came from all walks of life – he mentions 'skippers, ministers, doctors, teachers, joiners, plumbers, policemen, shoemakers, artists' – they were bound together in urban life by their consciousness of their Gaelic inheritance. They would send their children back 'home' during the long summer holidays. They were like a congregation of villages within the city, exchanging Gaelic nicknames and anecdotes as if they had never left their crops.

One is conscious in Glasgow of the surrounding country, for the hills come right down to its outskirts, and there is a constant awareness of how the Clyde leads to the firth and the open seas. The steam-puffers of the sea lochs maintained connections between Glasgow and its hinterland, and the most popular yarns of Edwardian Glasgow were the Para Handy stories of Neil Munro, himself an Argyll man from a Gaelic-speaking family. In these stories Munro wove a spell of nostalgic charm which captivated Glaswegians conscious of the Highland background so many possessed. They were the litarary equivalent of the most popular Glasgow diversion – a day 'doon the water', a boat-trip to Rothesay or Dunoon. Munro spent most of his working life as a journalist in the city, eventually as the editor of the *Glasgow*

Evening News from 1918 to 1927, but his heart remained in the Highlands where his best novels – *John Splendid* (1898) and *The New Road* (1914) – are set.

It is always easy to condemn nostalgia, and no doubt the nostalgic element in Munro's novels, itself a feature characteristic of most Scottish fiction of that time, both contributed to his popularity and corrupted his artistic intention. But it was not simply nostalgia which made the transplanted Gaels cling, as far as possible, to the patterns of life which belonged to their old homes. There was certainly undisguised nostalgia in the popular songs which John Roderick Bannerman composed for Hugh Roberton's famous Orpheus Choir – he wrote the music for 'Westering Home' and 'Come along, come along, let us foot it out together' – but it was perhaps something rather different when he decided to take over at the kitchen range and prepare 'a legacy from island days called *Bannach Gruthain*'. This was made from the head and neck of a big cod with a bannock made from oatmeal, chopped liver and onion stuffed in its mouth; it was then boiled and served with a white sauce, and in old age John M. Bannerman still remembered 'with relish the hunger-satisfying mixture of white fish and "cod haggis". Many an extra yard it must have carried me in a forward rush on the rugby field.'

The exiled Gaels would eat such meals in the same way as a Jewish family might delight in their own *gefilte-fish* and dumplings. They were not only a pleasure, but a means of maintaining continuity. The psychological strain of the translation from their rural culture to that of a modern industrial city was considerable. One method of combating it, of saving them from deracination and its disturbing consequences, was to carry as much as possible of their old life into the new one. So as many as possible took their holidays in the Highlands. They attended Gaelic churches and ceilidhs, they read Gaelic newspapers and magazines, many of them ephemeral, and wrote, acted and enjoyed Gaelic plays. John M. Bannerman recalled, with pleasure, the choirmaster of St Columba, A. B. Ferguson, as 'a splendid example of the Argyll Gael, a native of the Cowal district who worked in a Glasgow engineering shop and had two loves: first, shinty, and, second, Gaelic music. It was all a means of making urban life tolerable, and of humanising it. It worked for thousands of them, and as a corollary it humanised the city. The mood of Glasgow has been lightened by the Gaelic influence. However harsh life might be there, there has been a buoyancy and poetry absent from less fortunate cities. The proverbial hospitality of Glasgow may be attributed to the Gaelic element. Even the vertical social attachments, which create such a strong feeling that all its citizens belong to

Glasgow, and which do something to mitigate or nullify the stratification of society which has everywhere been the result of the industrial system, may, without fancifulness, be found to have their origins in the Gaelic concept of the community expressed in the idea of the clan. For there is indeed a sense in which Glaswegians are a clan.

One could go further and submit that the spirit of Glasgow, like that of Charles Rennie Mackintosh himself, is Celtic; and that Glasgow reproduces the Celtic spirit in its grandiosity and ardour, its improvidence and melancholy, its friendliness which can turn so abruptly to violence, its pride and its sentimentality, its warmth of family affections and its propensity to blood-feuds (for how else can the Rangers-Celtic rivalry be expressed?)

And one might add that the shift from individualistic to communal values, already remarked, has been brought about by the permeation of the Celtic strain. The Gaels, gathered in to the city to work as the lowest of the low, as hands and servants, have gradually imposed their values and subverted the previously dominant ethos of self-reliance and self-seeking.

CHAPTER TEN

CITY IN DECLINE

There were moments between the wars when it was possible to pretend that no essential change had taken place. The launching of the two great passenger liners, the *Queen Mary* and the *Queen Elizabeth*, from the John Brown yard in Clydebank, could feed the illusion that the nineteenth-century splendour was undimmed, for they were, undeniably, the greatest ships in the world. Likewise the Empire Exhibition of 1938, held in Bellahouston Park, fostered the impression that Glasgow remained the second city of the greatest Empire the world had ever seen, that the years since 1918 represented only a bad dream. It recalled the splendour of earlier exhibitions and reaffirmed the city's greatness; one of its attractions was a 17-ft model of the *Queen Elizabeth* due to be launched in a few months. Sir Percy Bates, the Chairman of the Cunard Company, which had ordered both the Queens, pandered to Glasgow's pride when he described them as examples of 'human audacity in steel'. And yet there was already a sense that time was running out: the Depression of the early 1930s, following on difficulties experienced by shipbuilding in the previous decade, after the immediate post-war boom fizzled out, had been so severe as to call the whole capitalist ethos into question, and to dim people's faith in Glasgow's future. In George Blake's novel, *The Shipbuilders* (1935), Leslie Pagan drives his invalid son down to the river and recounts family history to him, unfolding 'the splendour of the story his family had lived for generations'; yet, he reflects, 'It was written. The supreme glory had departed.'

The economic historian Sydney Checkland provided a metaphor to explain what was happening, had happened:

> The Upas tree of Java (*Antiaris Toxicaria*), entering European legend through Erasmus Darwin, was believed to have the power to destroy other growths for a radius of fifteen miles ... it is taken as a symbol of the heavy industry that so long dominated the economy and society of Glasgow .... The Upas tree of heavy engineering killed anything that sought to grow under its branches ... now the Upas tree, so long ailing, was decaying, its limbs falling

away one by one. Not only had it been inimical to other growths, it had, by an inversion of its condition before 1914, brought about limitation of its own performance.

No metaphor can adequately portray or account for any historical process, and the metaphor of the Upas tree may even have an Upas-like effect on the imagination. It is so dazzlingly convincing that it may inhibit the consideration of other factors in Glasgow's decline. It is also exaggerated.

Glasgow had other industries, despite the Upas tree. The Singer factory at Clydebank employed 3000 people making sewing-machines; the work-force was so large that a station called, simply, Singer, was opened on the city's suburban railway. The Wills tobacco factory on Alexandra Parade employed more people than many shipyards. Glasgow was also prominent in the production of mass-market textiles and clothing, food-processing and distilling, furniture-manufacture and confectionery. There was general understanding that light industries must be developed in Glasgow and the central belt of Scotland, and there was modest pride that some progress had been made in this direction in the decade before the Second World War. Nevertheless the 1930s were, in the economics of Glasgow as in the politics of Europe, the years the locusts ate: the 1935 Census of production found that car manufacture and electrical goods – two of the growth industries of the time – had only 2 per cent of their British work-force in Scotland.

The contrast with the nineteenth century was marked. Then Glasgow had found itself in the industrial avant-garde; its ships, locomotives, and bridges were the symbols of the new age. Now the equivalent symbols were to be found elsewhere: in the English Midlands and the light-industry towns – Slough, Stevenage and the like – that surrounded London. The moral effect was as significant as the material. It was not just that Glasgow failed to establish itself in the new world, not just that it lost the economic advantages of becoming a centre of the motor or electrical goods industries; it suffered also from its consciousness of failure. The mood of a city, necessarily intangible and hard to identify, is nevertheless potent. Glasgow had flourished while it felt itself to be in the van of progress; it withered when it seemed to be dragged at the tail of the twentieth-century chariot.

The Second World War Blitz on English cities such as London and Coventry and English ports, including Liverpool, Plymouth, Portsmouth and Hull, tends to obscure the fact that Clydeside suffered severe damage during two devastating night raids on 13 and 14 March 1941. The shipyards were crippled, houses destroyed and civilian casualties high. For the

Clydesiders it was a terrifying ordeal and a grim reminder that as a shipbuilding and industrial centre with a Rolls-Royce plant Glasgow had been selected by the Luftwaffe as a prime target.

The city suffered from circumstances over which it could have no control. Glasgow, along with Manchester and Liverpool, had been the classic free trade city; its market was the world, and its wealth had grown from its ability to service that market in an expanding global economy. But the 1930s saw world trade contract; in two years it fell by as much as a third. Alarmed and puzzled politicians responded to cries for Protection; and this did indeed aid the development of some of the new consumer industries which were thus cosseted against competition, especially from the United States. It did not help Glasgow, however. The conditions which had allowed the city to flourish had disappeared. They were replaced by new circumstances which imposed an inexorable decline on the city.

Edwin Muir identified what was happening with characteristic lucidity: 'A competitive system can provide for expansion; indeed expansion is a necessary condition for its smooth working. But it can make no provision for contraction.' The question was how Glasgow could adapt itself to an economy that had ceased, for the moment at any rate, to expand.

The most obvious, and optimistic, course was to attempt to divert economic activity into new areas which showed a capacity for growth even within an economy that was either stagnant or contracting. This was a natural and healthy response, but one fraught with difficulties. For example, Lord Weir, Chairman of the engineering firm G. & J. Weir, attempted to diversify in the early 1920s when poor trading conditions led to a drop in turnover which caused his firm's work-force to be cut by two-thirds. He tried to promote prefabricated steel houses which could be assembled on a building site by unskilled workers. The building trade naturally regarded this as a threat to their livelihood, and since the Weir houses were intended for local authorities, these came under pressure both from trade unions and from traditional house-building firms. A Government inquiry failed to find a compromise solution, and Weir's scheme was abandoned. The incident offered a clear example of the difficulties encountered in a contracting economy, in which new products could be promoted only at the expense of established ones.

The second course was to try to control contraction. This was the policy adopted by Sir James Lithgow, the shipbuilder who, during the war, had been Director of Merchant Shipping, acquiring in that post an understanding of how the economy might respond to planning; a thought which would have been anathema to the industrialists who had made Glasgow great on the principle of competition. It was something more in tune with the other side of the Glasgow experience – the collectivism fostered by the policy and activity of the Corporation.

Soon after the First World War Lithgow feared that the British shipbuilding industry was in danger of pricing itself out of the world market. This was not entirely the fault of the industry itself; the Government's decision to return to the Gold Standard in 1925 led to an overvalued pound. At the same time the unions were making wage demands which did not reflect the prosperity of the industry. Lithgow considered that 'when labour leaders instruct their members to welcome changes designed to reduce total costs and to work up to the reasonable capacity of their skill, realising that the laws of supply and demand in a democratically governed country are an ample safeguard against exploitation, there will be some hope of maintaining wages at a higher level'. This was a tune that could have been played at any time in the sixty years since; has indeed been played often enough. Lithgow, however, does not seem to have asked to what extent the employers were responsible for the reluctance of Labour to co-operate. Antagonism and distrust between employers and employed were the legacy of nineteenth-century experience, of the readiness of employers to discard labour, or cut wages, whenever profits dipped. Lithgow himself was a notably benevolent and conscientious man, but in general the Clyde's employers never understood the necessity of educating their work-force in the realities of economic forces. Being themselves unconvinced of the desirability of genuine co-operation, they were unable to convince the workers.

The failure to develop habits of mind suitable to twentieth-century industry was to play at least as great a part in Glasgow's decline as world economic conditions. It led to union militancy and defensiveness; to the preservation of protective work-systems, characterised by wasteful demarcation. It was easy to blame the unions for this and to accuse them of being myopically obstructive; but, though there was truth in such accusations, a greater responsibility perhaps lay with the employers who themselves retained a conception of the proper relationship between masters and men which more progressive countries and industries were abandoning.

Glasgow was caught in an outmoded economic system, but the city's plight was aggravated by the retention of intellectual assumptions which were equally antiquated. Care for welfare was rudimentary. When women workers were recruited to one yard during the Second World War, it was suggested that some of the men's lavatories should be converted for their use; the directors then discovered that the men had no lavatories. It was not surprising that antagonism and confrontation were the mood and mode of labour relations. They remained so long after the Second World War. An American academic, who studied Glasgow labour and management in the 1960s, observed that 'there often seems to be far more interest in the proportion between the wage level and profit than in absolute wages. A policy of rising wages which was accompanied by more rapidly rising profits would be interpreted as a trade union defeat.' He was right, but it was the employers who had set the tone in the first instance.

Lithgow's response to the crisis in shipbuilding was intellectually positive, though unpopular. Aware that some of the greatest firms – Beardmore's and Fairfield's, for example – were on the verge of bankruptcy, he approached the Governor of the Bank of England, Montagu Norman, the great advocate of financial retrenchment, with proposals for 'rationalisation'. The result was the formation, with support from the Bank, of the National Shipbuilders Security Ltd, with Lithgow as Chairman. It bought loss-making firms and then 'sterilised' them. In this way construction capacity was cut, and the available work shared out among a smaller number of yards. Lithgow provided much of the finance for this rescue operation himself, but naturally his methods aroused opposition from the unions, more conscious of the destructive elements of the scheme than of the benefits it brought to surviving yards, of the jobs lost than of the other jobs saved. In 1932 Lithgow took over Beardmore's altogether, assuming responsibility for Fairfield's two years later. By the late 1930s the rearmament programme was bringing new orders to the Clyde and the crisis facing shipbuilding there was apparently averted.

Alas, it was only postponed. There was a brief post-war boom, as replacement vessels were required for ships destroyed or damaged during six years of war. But this was over by the mid-1950s. The Clyde was then brought up hard against reality. Demand from the Royal Navy was limited; only Yarrow's flourished on the strength of naval contracts. The passenger ship market was disappearing, for air travel was replacing sea travel, and, despite Weir's early involvement in aircraft manufacture, Glasgow had remained committed to ships, not aircraft. Merchant shipping could still be profitable, but the Clyde was now bedevilled by restrictive practices, distrust of innovation, and the insistence on parity of wage rates, which were already higher than those of many foreign competitors; parity ensured that workers in unprofitable, or dubiously profitable, yards, should be paid as much as those in the more successful ones. In desperation, managements tendered for contracts at prices which brought no profit, and offered delivery dates which they could not meet. Consequently, winning a contract might prove more damaging than failure to win one, for it often only increased the indebtedness of the firm. John Brown's of Clydebank lost £3 million on the *Kungsholm*, the difference between the contracted price and the actual cost of construction.

The 1960s would see the Clyde lurching from one crisis to the next. Its industrial troubles dominated the news, and poisoned the atmosphere. The ironies of historical development were fully apparent. Clyde-built had been a synonym for quality; now the Clyde seemed to represent all that was worst in British industry: restrictive work practices; obsolete ideologies; weak, unimaginative, and increasingly desperate management; inefficiency; over-manning; short-sightedness; the absence of any intelligent sense of direc-tion. Glasgow, which had flourished as the supreme example of a free market economy, now struggled along with the help of subsidies supplied directly by the State, indirectly by those other parts of Britain which had adapted better to twentieth-century realities.

Ill-considered expediency succeeded ill-considered expediency. This was not surprising, for the imminence of disaster precluded reflection. So, even promising schemes, such as the reconstruction of Fairfield's in 1965, with the support of the Government, unions and private finance, under the leadership of the successful industrialist Sir Iain Stewart, were abandoned before they had time to prove themselves. Indeed this particular reconstruc-tion made things worse in other Clyde yards, for unions successfully demanded that Fairfield's rates should be paid there also. In any case the experiment lasted only three years before the Fairfield yard was subsumed in Upper Clyde Shipbuilders (UCS), a consortium formed irrationally from John Brown, Yarrow, Connell, Fairfield and Alexander Stephen, yards which had little in common except location, which would resist intelligent re-organisation, and which employed more than a quarter of all British shipbuilding workers, some 14,000 men. Within eighteen months more than £20 million of public money had been advanced to UCS. It soon disappeared; by June 1971 it was evident that the rationalisation was a failure. Yarrow, still successful in its concentration on naval vessels, became independent again. A liquidator was appointed for UCS; it looked like the end of shipbuilding on the Upper Clyde.

What followed was a drama which almost immediately created its own legend. The workers led by two shop stewards, Jimmy Airlie and Jimmy Reid, both then Communists, staged a 'work-in'. They occupied the yards and continued to work on the existing contracts. The liquidator, Robert Smith, co-operated with them, continuing to pay them out of UCS assets. The Conservative Government of Edward Heath was persuaded that public order in Glasgow could not be guaranteed, and so reversed its declared policy of leaving 'lame duck' industries to their fate. Another rescue operation, the most elaborate and expensive of all, was launched. Govan Shipbuilders was formed from Fairfield's and Alexander Stephen's, with Scotstoun Marine (formerly Connell's) as a subsidiary. John Brown, inefficient, disorderly and expensive, was sold to the Texan company, Marathon Manufacturing, to build oil platforms for the North Sea. (Within a few years Marathon would withdraw, the yard then being divided between a French company UIE and a new firm, John Brown Engineering.) This new rescue cost at least £72 million, almost £60 million going to Govan Shipbuilders, and £12 million to Marathon. Even this was not the end, for more money and more restructuring would still be required. There would be more changes of ownership, more cries for help, more lamentation over failure.

And yet, in an important sense, it was the end. The UCS crisis was the nadir. It saw the once-proud industry reduced to the status of a despised and widely resented beggar. Shipbuilding might still survive on the Clyde, but illusions had been shattered. No one contemplating the fiascos associated with the industry could any longer pretend that Glasgow's wealth and prosperity depended on it. No one could imagine that its revival was the essential condition for Glasgow's revival. The period of two centuries during which Glasgow's prosperity had risen from the waters of the Clyde was over. Sydney Checkland observed that 'like Venice, Glasgow had her empires *da mar* and *terra firma*, each part of the other; in Glasgow's case they were wedded by the steam engine'. Now, with the heavy industry of the hinterland itself heading for oblivion, with shipbuilding curtailed and apparently doomed, Glasgow was faced with the prospect of becoming, like Venice, a city living on memories of departed glory. The song of the Clyde was stilled.

There was another sense in which the UCS affair marked the end of illusion. Appropriately the act which signalled that end itself took the form of illusion. Glasgow, or part of Glasgow, had cherished its myth, its self-image, as a potentially revolutionary city. The days of Maclean and Red Clydeside were celebrated in song and alcoholic conversation. They were recalled, with advantages, during the UCS work-in. But the work-in itself showed this to be nonsense, for it was made possible by the willingness of the liquidator, himself a bourgeois chartered accountant, to co-operate with Airlie and Reid. The work-in was distinguished less by the expression of revolutionary, or even defiant, sentiments, than by intelligent awareness of the limits of what might be achieved. Satisfaction might be derived from the reversal of Government policy which the support of shipbuilding on the Upper Clyde entailed, but all this meant was that the Heath Government had been persuaded to behave like every British Government between 1929 and 1979, and sacrifice a coherent economic policy to perceived social necessity. It was symptomatic of the end of revolutionary illusion which the UCS settlement entailed that within a few years Jimmy Reid should have become a newspaper columnist expressing views held on the moderate wing of the Labour Party, while Jimmy Airlie, as an official of the Amalgamated Engineering Union, should have been instrumental in trying to bring the Ford Motor Company to Dundee and ready to sign a single-union no-strike deal to secure this. Inasmuch as Clydeside was ever Red, the UCS work-in represented the last flicker of the embers.

The Glasgow Labour Party had long eschewed the romanticism of revolutionary rhetoric. It had settled into a comfortable role as a douce managerial organisation. The principal figure in this development was Patrick Dollan, later knighted, as all Lord Provosts of Glasgow were. Dollan was an Irish Catholic who started as an associate of Wheatley and Maxton and as a member of the ILP. Unlike his friends he concentrated on municipal politics; unlike them, therefore, he enjoyed more power than reputation. He was the type of machine-politician more common perhaps in the United States than in Britain. He understood the limited aims of the working-class voter: he realised that the provision of better housing and job security could attach the loyalty of the electorate. If he ever had a real desire to change the system, he soon lost it. It was his task to effect reforms that would make the system work tolerably and more fairly. He operated within the limits of the possible; in economic terms this meant little more than attaching 'fair wage' clauses to municipal contracts and in setting up the Corporation's own direct labour department. Beyond that, Dollan established the principle that local government existed to try to extract largesse from the national government.

Within the city, he was the natural heir of the old traditions of the authoritarian Corporation. Indeed it is hard to see any break even in policy. The Housing Acts of 1919, 1923 and 1924 had all encouraged the Corporation to embark on house-building programmes. It was then dominated by Moderates who, though not attached to any political party in their capacity as councillors, would have voted Conservative or Liberal. Labour did not achieve power till 1933, and then as a result of a split in the right-wing vote, occasioned by the arrival of the demogogic, but short-lived, Scottish Protestant League.

Housing estates were built on green-field sites on the outskirts of the city.

The two largest were Mosspark and Knightswood, which were spaciously and ambitiously designed. Tenements were associated with slums, and low-density housing was favoured. Knightswood indeed bore some resemblance to the garden city proposed by Edwardian housing theorists: it had much open space, and provided a library, public hall and parades of shops. Naturally, such an ornament to the city required carefully chosen tenants, who were mostly skilled workers or white-collar employees. Many indeed were employed by the Corporation itself; by the mid-1930s there were some 40,000 municipal employees of one kind or another. In theory this removal of the 'respectable' poor to these new estates left their old houses vacant for people who might aspire to respectability. Other new estates such as Blackhill, built near the centre, were less highly regarded. The quality of housing was poorer there, and the density higher. Blackhill became a depository for unsatisfactory council tenants, decanted from the old slums into a scheme which soon became a slum itself, if a less 'picturesque' one. Blackhill was to provide an unhappy model for post-war developments in Castlemilk, Drumchapel and Easterhouse.

Without the intention ever perhaps being explicitly formed, the Labour majority on the Corporation found itself engaged, with, it must be said, the support of other parties, on a course of social engineering. It was a form of benevolent authoritarianism: council officials were granted enormous power to shape people's lives. Those tenants of whom they approved were allotted 'Ordinary' houses in the better new estates; those who were found wanting were assigned to 'Rehousing' houses at Blackhill and its successors. The Victorian distinction between the Respectable and the Disreputable Poor was thus confirmed by the party which had set itself to abolish poverty. The new estates lacked the organic character of Gorbals, without the social mix which had been created by the haphazard arrival of immigrants. A notorious street in Blackhill lodged between 1948 and 1960 20 delinquent offenders per 100 houses of whom 29 per cent became adult criminals.

Glasgow's housing problems were so enormous that it was understandable that the remedies sought had an improvised character. There was no comprehensive view, though a city which had developed naturally in accordance with market forces was now, in theory, being restructured rationally. One consequence of this was the control exercised by the Corporation; of 76,360 houses built in the city between the wars, only 9106 were privately built. There was a natural suspicion of private landlords, engendered by the experience of the slums; but the contrast with English cities where building firms were putting up streets of semi-detached bungalows to be sold to private buyers was marked. The Glasgow housing policy reflected the defensive mood forced on the city by economic decline; it was itself a form of protection, displaying a distrust of the market.

It was pursued, even intensified, after the Second World War. The need for housing was desperate: more than 80,000 families were on the waiting-lists for council housing. One response was overspill, the decanting of part of the city's population to New Towns or to old towns such as Haddington and Hawick which were willing to accept them. The Clyde Valley Plan of 1946 had urged 'a planned decentralisation of both population and industry ... in the interests of the city and the region as a whole'. This was a logical response to the density of population within the boundaries of the city: in some areas there were 700 people to the acre in 1945; the Scottish Office considered an acceptable figure to be 160. Unfortunately many who left were skilled workers; the New Town of East Kilbride in 1966 had a ratio of 14.6 skilled men to each unskilled man; the Glasgow ratio was only 3:1.

Meanwhile the Corporation built its huge working-class dormitories on the outskirts. The high ideals which had informed Knightswood were not evident there. These estates absorbed some 10 per cent of Glasgow's population. The houses were better, but the life was in many respects worse. There were, at first, few, if any, amenities: an 1890 Corporation resolution forbade the provision of public houses on Corporation property. The desire for housing was so great that the absence of a pub was not felt at once; but when the immediate pleasure of the house had been exhausted, the deprivation was realised. The policy of selective assignment continued. By the mid-1960s it was clear that the Corporation had involuntarily created new slums and imposed a system of segregation at the same time.

The last fling was made in the 1960s with the provision of high-rise flats. By the end of the decade the Corporation's Housing Management Department had 15,000 'high-rise *units*' (my italics) on its books along with 121,500 'low-rise' ones. This was a notable development. It changed not only the city's skyline but the pattern of urban life. The Glasgow experience had caused people to set a high value on local communities. The old slums had been made tolerable for many – and glow rosily in retrospect – precisely because of the vigour of communal experience. This was hard to reproduce in the multi-storeys. Moreover, it is doubtful whether the 'style' of living which high-rise flats impose is ever suited to the poor; perhaps it is only tolerable for those with the personal mobility which affluence makes possible. In particular, mothers with small children suffered nervous strain in the tower blocks. In as much as the high-rises offered a solution of a sort to housing accountants' problems, they created new ones. Loneliness, depression, alienation, delinquency, vandalism were soon regarded as common consequences of tower-block living. The change was real; the improvement dubious.

For all these failures, however, the economic decline of the period 1919–70, which was itself only comparative, in that by the end of this period the standard of living of the average Glaswegian was considerably higher than that of his equivalent after the First World War, was not mirrored in the field of social policy. To this extent, indeed, Glasgow reproduced, as it had done in the nineteenth century, the experience of Britain as a whole. Compared with other cities and countries, Glasgow and Britain could both be seen to have fallen away from the position they enjoyed in 1914. The Empire had gone, and with it economic leadership. In both Britain as a whole, and Glasgow in particular, the self-confidence, energy and inventiveness which had distinguished the previous century of vigorous growth had faded and withered. Yet this half-century was also a time of steady social progress. At its end the great majority of Glasgow's population was better housed, better fed, better educated, enjoyed comparatively better health, more leisure and a greater variety of opportunities for recreation than it had at the beginning. At the very least this improvement meant that when Glasgow's economic fortunes revived, the revival started from a higher base. But it meant much more than that; it meant that Glasgow was a better city than it had been in its heyday. In 1935, in the depths of the Depression, Edwin Muir had asked, 'How is this collapsing city to be put on its feet again?' The answer had not been found by the early 1970s, but the collapse had at least been arrested.

Muir insisted that 'the fundamental realities of Glasgow are economic'. He was right. He also remarked that 'a modern city is strictly inconceivable, on account of the myriad activities, attitudes, styles of life it contains'; and this is also true. He added, economic realities aside, 'the other aspects of modern towns have become journalism', which means, I suppose, that they can be rendered only by impressionistic sketches, in which a single snapshot of experience is assigned a representative quality. And yet it is such snapshots which give life to appreciation of a city. Muir himself realised this: his account of Glasgow, for all his insistence to the contrary, is made up of impressions:

It was a very hot bright day when I went down to see the shipyards that once in my life I had passed every morning. The weather had been good for several weeks, and all the men I saw were tanned and brown as if they had just come back from their summer holidays. They were standing in the usual groups, or walking by twos or threes, slowly, for one felt as one looked at them that the world had not a single message to send them on, and that for them to hasten their steps would have meant a sort of madness. Perhaps at some time the mirage of work glimmered at the extreme horizon of their minds; but one could see by looking at them that they were no longer deceived by such false pictures.

That is journalism, and a sketch as instructive and illuminating as a picture of a motionless crane thrusting up into a Clydeside mist.

The long years of Glasgow's economic failure have inevitably done more to form the character of modern Glaswegians – and one's own impression of that character – than memories of the nineteenth-century triumphs. A boarded-up factory with willow-herb growing out through cracks in the walls or a tenement terrace awaiting demolition that seems endlessly postponed speak more eloquently of Glasgow than the magnificent tombs of its Necropolis rising behind the Cathedral. Yet even in Glasgow's worst decades the character has always seemed positive. The travel writer, H.V. Morton, who visited the city in 1928, called Glasgow, 'Scotland's anchor to reality. Lacking her, Scotland would be a backward country lost in poetic memories and at enmity with an age in which she was playing no part.' It is an interesting judgement, if partly because the second sentence might have been applied to Glasgow itself in the subsequent half-century. The first one is sound enough; an anchor to reality.

Morton found in Glasgow 'a Transatlantic alertness which no city in England possesses. There is no half-heartedness about Glasgow ... and it is not a suburban city like London.' He was impressed by what he called its 'close-togetherness', by the absence of frontiers between classes. In the same street you would see 'the biggest assembly of bowler hats in Britain and the slow walk of a hatless woman from a neighbouring tenement bearing, much as the kangaroo bears its young, a tiny face in the fold of a thick tartan shawl'. He decided that 'in no other city of this magnitude do more people know each other, at least by sight. To know a man by sight in Glasgow is to ask him to have a coffee at eleven a.m. If the Clyde ever runs dry, sufficient coffee is consumed in Glasgow every morning to float the biggest Cunarder yet built.'

Much of what he says remains true. The 'close-togetherness' of Glasgow is still apparent. Glasgow likes to see itself as 'American' in its restlessness, in its willingness to knock down buildings, and to experiment, but it is European in its powerful civic sense. In this it resembles an Italian city, evoking a powerful loyalty from its citizens and being, in Morton's word, 'self-centred'. Even today some three-quarters of those who attend its two

Universities are from Glasgow proper or from the Glasgow conurbation; the bourgeoisie belong to Glasgow in a way that finds its equivalent in Italian cities, but which is unusual in England. The majority have lived all their lives in Glasgow or its surroundings, and are – which again is unusual elsewhere – happy to do so. Glasgow is still predominantly a working-class city; yet it is one to which the middle class is passionately attached. It is not only self-centred; it is self-sufficient.

For many, the characteristic Glasgow figure became the 'wee hard man', the 'wee bauchle', swaggering on bandy legs, given to sudden outbursts of violence, quick-witted, humorous, lachrymosely sentimental in drink, proud, democratic, a family man who yet preferred to live most of his time in an exclusively male world. Few conformed exactly to this stereotype, and the man who gave the world the song that exemplified it, Will Fyffe, himself came from Dundee; yet 'I belong tae Glasgow' was one of those popular songs that succeeded because it perfectly captured a characteristic mood.

Glasgow could seem a city given over to a celebration of maleness. Though by the 1920s a high proportion of women went out to work, so that in the next decade it was common enough to find a wife working while her man was unemployed, the Glaswegian working ideal was harshly masculine: the man in his dungarees, with the head of a spanner and tightly folded newspaper sticking out of his pocket, moving with purposeful slightly rolling gait to the yard. The leisure activities of the adult male, after he had grown out of the stage of frequenting the dance-halls in search of a partner, were exclusive: the public-house, the football match on a Saturday afternoon, to which he went straight after his morning's work without returning home. The role models were stereotypes, easily recognisable. The respectable young man found his in the yard where he worked, in the masters of the trade to which he was apprenticed; his less reputable counterpart identified with the 'hard man' who might dominate, and terrorise, his own little patch of the city.

Their heroes were to be found in the world of professional sport. For men who were bound to their present circumstances for life, and who generally indeed had little desire to effect any substantial alteration in these circumstances, sport fed the imagination with dreams of glory. The intense rivalry between Rangers and Celtic might distress socially conscious moralists, and the occasional outbursts of violence which were provoked might seem evidence that the rivalry enflamed sectarian hatreds; but it is, at least, possible that football acted as a safety-valve, so enabling hatred to dissipate itself in comparatively harmless fashion. In any case Rangers and Celtic existed in symbiotic association; they could not have done without each other. They were thesis and antithesis, and the synthesis was Scottish football, for the popular conception of the two clubs reproduced the contradictions of Glasgow's character which nevertheless came together in a coherent whole. Celtic were Catholic, Irish and Highland, gallant, inventive, artistic, 'in victory more than men, in defeat less than women': Rangers, Protestant, dour, hard, practical, efficient. Rangers believed in their divine right to success even in periods of failure; Celtic viewed even their greatest triumphs with a certain wondering incredulity. Individuals contradicted the stereotypes: Rangers had their artists such as Alan Morton, Torry Gillick, Ian MacMillan, and pre-eminently, Jim Baxter; Celtic their hard men, their fiercely efficient players: their greatest goal-scorer Jimmy McGrory, wing-halves such as Bobby Evans and, in modern times, Roy Aitken. Nevertheless, temperamentally, the stereotypes were just, and, as I say, at least as complementary as they were contradictory. To an outsider it seemed that Celtic represented the familial side of Glasgow, Rangers the city's business ethics, that Celtic incarnated the feminine principle, Rangers the masculine one; take either club away, and the city would not only be diminished, but out of kilter. Their rivalry was necessary to make Glasgow whole.

Glasgow was equally entranced by success and failure; both appealed to the city's lust for drama. For this reason the city's music-halls, the Empire and the Pavilion, were among the hardest to play in Britain, and among the most rewarding. The audience was robust, sharply critical, but also sentimental and outgoing; it expected to be able to enter into a warm relationship with performers, and reacted angrily when this was not established. It delighted in seeing its own face in the glass, and cherished those – Will Fyffe, Tommy Lorne, Tommy Morgan, Jimmy Logan, Rikki Fulton and Jack Milroy, Stanley Baxter, Billy Connolly who let it do so.

The duality of Glasgow's nature received expression from its heroes. In the worst years of the Depression it seemed almost necessary that glittering success should lead to abysmal failure. The career of the champion boxer Benny Lynch delighted and satisfied, even while it aroused pity and terror. He was born in 1910, in the slums. He grew up in the Depression, when one man in three in the poor quarters was out of work, and one child in ten died at birth or in infancy. He was very small, a natural flyweight, differentiated from thousands of other boys only by his speed of foot and fist, the extraordinary nature of his innate ability to fight. Unlike most flyweights, he possessed a genuine knock-out punch; he could punch as hard and as crisply as boxers two stones heavier, and this ability took him to the world title. In this achievement he seemed to strike a blow for all the deprived and dispossessed; he was something more than a hero, he was an incarnation of all that they had dreamed.

But having arrived, having fulfilled the dream, he had no means of surviving; the dream achieved, he had nothing with which to sustain him. A member of a peasantry thrust by economic circumstance into proletarian existence, he was lost as soon as he could no longer identify exactly with the world that identified with him. He took refuge in the bottle. He neglected training, entered the ring unready to fight, and lost his essential gift – the ability to time a punch. He did not know how to accept the help which was offered him. His admirers shrank back from the spectacle of his decline, appalled. They had seen in his glory the expression of their own vitality and refusal to submit to the indignities which economics forced on them; now they recognised their own weakness in his disintegration. Their rage, or rather their horror, was that of Caliban, forced to confront his own image. Benny Lynch's fall was rapid, though slow and agonising compared to his rise. He was dead at the age of thirty-three, a miserable derelict. His story was exemplary; it offered the authentic tragedy of the Glasgow slums.

In the streets Glasgow might seem a male-dominated city. It was different in the home. Every respectable Glasgow family, every family that aspired to respectability, was a matriarchy. Here too Glasgow resembled an Italian city, and, as in an Italian family, the mother's rule rested more heavily on her daughters. Boys were spoiled, excused any domestic tasks; it was recognized that their time would come when they were expected to be breadwinners in their turn. A respectable woman's life was a constant struggle to maintain standards, a long war against dirt and disease, in which there was no victory possible except the fact of survival.

CHAPTER ELEVEN

REVIVAL

The perception of Glasgow has changed in the last decade. The failing city has become – in parts – the flourishing one. Muir's question – 'How is this collapsing city to be put on its feet again?' – looks antiquated and absurd. The thing has been done. Yet it is hard to determine how or why this has happened. This is partly because we are too close to it. In 1983, when Dr Michael Kelly was Lord Provost, the city's public relations advisers coined the slogan, 'Glasgow's Miles Better'. It was easy at first to dismiss this as advertising froth. Yet Mr Happy's greeting stuck, imprinting itself in the general consciousness. It did so because it aroused an awakening understanding that Glasgow was indeed miles better than it had been. Gradually it was realised that the city had come through, that it was emerging into sunlight from a long journey through the dark. And this realisation held good even though Glasgow had suffered severely in the recession of the early 1980s, even though unemployment in some parts of the city reached the appalling levels of half a century earlier.

The transformation was abrupt. In 1981 Alasdair Gray's novel *Lanark* was published. 'Glasgow is a magnificent city,' one character says. 'Why do we hardly ever notice that?' 'Because nobody imagines living here,' his friend replies. He goes on to explain: 'Think of Florence, Paris, London, New York. Nobody visiting them is a stranger because he's already visited them in paintings, novels, history books and films. But if a city hasn't been used by an artist not even the inhabitants live there imaginatively .... Imaginatively Glasgow exists as a music-hall song and a few bad novels. That's all we've given to the world outside. It's all we've given to ourselves ...' He overstated the case; there had been good novels and good paintings, there were great buildings. Yet there was substance in the argument; it was a long time since Glasgow had lived fruitfully in the imagination, even of its own citizens. It was a long time since they had felt for their city anything more than an ironic affection, tinged with despair. One of the best Glasgow novels of the post-war years, *The Dear Green Place* (1966) by Archie Hind, had taken as its theme the stultifying effect of Glasgow on the imagination. Its hero was a working-class man who strove to be a writer, and found himself continually thwarted by the realities of daily life. In Alan Spence's stories the bleakest element was not the material circumstances of his characters' lives, but the manner in which these circumstances constricted, dulled and threatened to kill the imaginative faculty. Now there was a sense in which Gray's imaginative novel represented a liberation. His Glasgow needed to apologise to nobody. Even if the original charge in that snatch of dialogue quoted above was overstated, it was a charge that could never be made again. Interestingly, since *Lanark* was published, Gray's friend James Kelman has published *A Disaffection* (1989), *Greyhound for Breakfast* (1987), *The Busconductor Hines* (1984), *A Chancer* (1985) and *Not Not While the Giro* (1983) which all treat of areas of Glasgow life which remain deprived and which may fairly be thought to have been untouched by any sense of Glasgow's renaissance. Yet these books are themselves evidence of that renaissance, for they are distinguished by a confident and muscular imagination, an awareness, too, that the world of which Kelman is writing has a validity and importance equal to any. They are books notably free from any sense of inferiority. They make none of the ingratiating concessions to the reader which are a mark of fiction whose author doubts its worth.

Art of one kind or another has played an important part in the revival of Glasgow. The public manifestations are obvious: the city is the home of Scottish Opera, the Scottish National Orchestra, and Scottish Ballet; its Citizens Theatre, under the triumvirate of Giles Havergal, Robert David Macdonald, and Philip Prowse, has won a European reputation for the audacity and brilliance of its productions. There is sometimes the objection, even in Glasgow, that there is nothing characteristically Scottish or Glaswegian about it. The charge is justified and misguided: the Citizens has flourished precisely because it has never accepted the limitations which the adoption of a specifically Scottish persona would have imposed on it. It has refused to be bound within assumptions which, in the current context, would condemn it to a certain provinciality. Instead it presumed to suppose that Glasgow and the world can speak to each other on equal terms. This policy was pursued long before anyone thought Glasgow was recovering; it played its own part in effecting that recovery.

The part played by the long-delayed opening of the Burrell Collection in attracting attention to Glasgow is well known. The Collection immediately established itself as one of Scotland's two principal tourist attractions, along with Edinburgh Castle. This was serviceable; twenty years earlier scarcely any tourists thought to come to Glasgow; its associations were repellent. Now Glasgow, like every great historic city of Europe, recognises the value of tourism to the local economy though, of course, it is possible that if Glasgow becomes too tourist-oriented, it will lose much of the gritty integrity that plays such a large part of its appeal in the first place. The effect of the Burrell Collection was, however, far more profound. More than any other single event its opening changed the perception of Glasgow. It elevated the city in public consciousness, in the consciousness of its own citizens as well as outsiders. In retrospect, the long delay in finding a suitable site for the Collection, a delay which was then regarded as humiliating evidence of the City Fathers' indifference to art, now appears providential. It is inconceivable that the 'Burrell effect' would have operated in the same way if the award-winning museum had been opened twenty years earlier.

The seeds of revival were sown in the bad years. No city makes a complete break with its past, any more than an individual person can. Our tendency to divide history into sharply defined periods can be mischievous. Just as a historian casting back can find evidence of imminent decline even in Glasgow's years of glory, so one can see now that what seemed like desperate or fruitless or mistaken ventures prepared the way for resurgence.

The decision taken on the basis of a Highway Plan presented in 1965 to drive motorways through the heart of Glasgow was bitterly opposed by many. It involved the destruction of some 7000 houses and the displacement of whole communities. It seemed a mistaken policy to adopt in a city which had – and still has – an unusually low level of car ownership. It destroyed the sense of wholeness which had characterised Glasgow, and isolated surviving communities between soulless highways. It made Glasgow for ten years or more resemble a city which had suffered extensive bomb damage. The scars have not yet healed.

Nevertheless the motorways represented one of the most important elements in the renaissance. The benefits were both practical and psychological. In the first place, they provided rapid and convenient movement from one part of the city to another, and into and out of the city as well. At a time when London is coming to a halt, the advantages of this are ever more evident. You have only to see the expression on the face of a London businessman who is told by his Glasgow counterpart that he can be at Glasgow Airport in twenty minutes from any point in the City Centre to realise this, as the Londoner's initial incredulity gives way to envy. But perhaps the psychological benefit was still more important: they – together with the renovated Underground, promptly labelled the 'Clockwork Orange' – restored to Glaswegians the sense that their city was on the move.

They restored the sense of adventure which had been a characteristic of the nineteenth-century city. They signalled that acceptance of fate had been replaced by a willingness to challenge it.

The motorways also represented something new. It was no longer a matter of repairing the damage caused by Industrialism, as slum clearance and re-housing had been. Instead they offered a clean break with the past. Perhaps most important of all, their construction marked an end to the obsession with the Clyde. The city had grown up, and grown rich, along the river; now the river itself was spanned by fast roads leading away from it. Their symbolism was as important as their physical reality. They offered a new way of thinking, an understanding that, if Glasgow was to recover, it must find new sources of wealth; that the great days of the great ships had gone, and would not return.

Perhaps this realisation was the most important factor in the renaissance. For more than half a century Glasgow had struggled first to maintain, then to revive, its nineteenth-century greatness. Now it had admitted that this was impossible. It had worshipped at the shrine of the Upas tree, long after the gods had slipped away. Now it had accepted that the old religion was dead. Attempts would still be made – and rightly made – to maintain shipbuilding and engineering; but Glasgow's wealth would never depend on them again. Gradually the realisation grew that there were other ways to prosper. It was seen that the days of great manufacturing cities in Europe were over; scarcely a single prosperous European city any longer depended primarily on large-scale heavy industry; instead, though they contained manufacturing industry, they were increasingly dominated by service industries. Why should Glasgow be different?

Paradoxically, the reviving confidence which expressed itself in the acceptance of novelty also encouraged conservation. The New Glasgow Society was founded in 1963, appropriately holding its first meeting in Alexander Thomson's St Vincent Street Church. The name was significant: the society proposed to preserve the old in order to make the new. It became a tireless campaigner for development which respected the Victorian city Glaswegians had inherited, while producing a stream of plans for redevelopment which was imaginative and intelligent. It played a great part in arousing people's consciousness of the beauty and nature of the Victorian city, and in creating a fuller awareness of Glasgow's unique qualities. The rehabilitation of the old Merchant City, lying between George Square and the High Street, was to be a logical extension in the 1980s of their pioneering work. When it happened, there were complaints about parvenus, but a thriving city needs such trendsetters. The tobacco lords set the pace in their time.

Besides, whatever social stratification was occasioned by this movement of young middle-class professionals back into the city centre, it was less than had been achieved by the city's housing department over the preceding decades. As Checkland put it:

> It is necessary to face the fact that in Glasgow, as elsewhere, the massive public housing sector has not reduced but has accelerated social polarisation, carrying it far beyond what was present under market conditions. This has been the result of constant sifting of so many families over a long period under a series of rules. This perverse outcome has had a further result: it has, by concentration, heightened the statistical appearance of deprivation by generating very bad areas.

One result has been to create an artificial housing shortage because vacant houses appear in areas to which other council dwellers do not wish to be transferred, or in which young couples do not want to start married life. In the early 1980s as many as a quarter of the houses in estates such as Drumchapel and Castlemilk were unoccupied. One encouraging feature of the decade has, however, been the development of more mixed housing, partly because private-sector builders have at last been encouraged to construct houses for sale in the inner city, partly because of the growth of Housing Associations, and partly because of the sale of council houses to their tenants.

It was natural that for half a century the Corporation should concentrate its energies and resources on housing. It could not do otherwise given the scale of the problem. If it was frequently insensitive, if many of the estates it built were inadequate or undesirable, it did effect genuine improvements. It did so, however, at great cost, both financial and social. The rebuilding programme was expensive; business and domestic rates were high, partly because, naturally enough in view of the income levels of so many council tenants, it was Labour policy to keep rents low. The consequences were unfortunate: many businesses and many of the middle class moved out of the city. By 1975 57 per cent of Glasgow's housing stock was in public ownership: some 158,000 houses out of 275,000.

The last fifteen years have seen a change of direction. The phrase 'urban renewal' has taken on a wider meaning. It has been realised that the provision of houses is not enough in itself, and that a city can flourish only if a variety of business is encouraged and provided for. The catalyst for this has been the Scottish Development Agency (SDA), about to be re-labelled Scottish Enterprise. The Gear (Glasgow Eastern Area Renewal) Project, set up by the Labour Government in 1976, and co-ordinated by the SDA, was the most ambitious attempt at comprehensive redevelopment. The area covered the old industrial centre of Glasgow: Shettleston, Dalmarnock, Bridgeton and Parkhead, where a population of almost 150,000 had been reduced by a third in the last quarter of a century. Those that remained had very low incomes; fewer than one in five households could afford to own a car, though this figure was less noteworthy than it seems since the area contained a very high proportion of pensioners and single-parent families. Physical renewal was the easiest part of the enterprise, and the most completely achieved; economic renewal was more difficult, and was in any case retarded by the recession of the early 1980s. Nevertheless, GEAR was a positive example of what might be achieved by co-operation between Government agencies, the local authorities and the private sector. Its example was to be followed, at both city-wide and local level. Glasgow Action was formed, a high-powered group containing many of the leading businessmen of the city, academics and councillors, in order to stimulate and promote development. At a local level, Govan Initiative Ltd, with its headquarters in Rangers' Ibrox Stadium, was formed to facilitate the redevelopment of an area impoverished by the decline of shipbuilding. The 1988 Garden Festival was held on reclaimed dockland, evidence of the determination to make new use of the river; other docks were converted into waterfront housing, and the same thing is happening along the old Forth/Clyde Canal. By the end of the century Glasgow will have experienced as great a physical change as took place between 1920 and 1970. This time, however, the changes will please the eye and elate the spirits. The physical transformation of Glasgow is an essential element in its moral renovation.

The character of a city is intangible; yet we all apply adjectives which suggest that we can identify a difference of character between one place and another. In the same way all cities spawn myths, float on myths. Some of those which have attached themselves to Glasgow have been damaging. There was the Gorbals myth, though there were always worse parts of the city, and in the 1930s the new housing estate of Blackhill, a dormitory rather than a complete community, was accounted far more dangerous territory. But it was Gorbals which impressed itself on the public imagination, giving Glasgow a dark glamour like Chicago's, and a reputation which the local hard men thought themselves obliged to sustain. The myth was reinforced by the novel, *No Mean City*, with its lurid picture of the razor gangs and pitched battles in the street; the novel made the worst of slum life stand for the whole. Perhaps, however, the real reason for the power and durability of the myth was that Gorbals stood within ten minutes' walk of the City Chambers; this seemed to bring violence right up to the steps of the civic authority.

There was the myth of Red Clydeside, which flattered the working class by assuring them of a revolutionary zeal scarcely manifested in reality. Dickson McCunn's observation that the working-man's 'notion of reality' was 'often just a short working-day and looking on at a football match on Saturday' might be nearer to the truth, but quite lacked the potency of memories of John Maclean and George Square in 1919.

There was the myth of the hard-headed businessman, which flattered the middle class and bolstered its confidence even while it was, or should have been, clear that some such businessmen were failing the city. This myth was carried over to the professional classes. Again, in *Huntingtower*, when Mr McCunn approaches his lawyer to find out about the eponymous property in Ayrshire, the lawyer remarks 'caustically': 'Usual Edinburgh way of doing business,' when he encounters some uncertainty as to the exact status of the property; but it was Edinburgh, not Glasgow, which engrossed the bulk of Scottish legal business, just as, in the 1970s Edinburgh stole a march on the larger city in the provision of financial services.

There was the myth of the warm-hearted city, which Glaswegians loved to cherish. Naturally, all these myths contained truth. They would not have flourished otherwise. The Glasgow working class did have a sense of its own importance, which derived in part from its awareness that it stood in the front rank of the labour movement in opposition to the excesses of capitalism. But it owed less to a revolutionary tradition than to the older awareness that the heavy industries of Clydeside provided the basis of Britain's nineteenth-century wealth and imperial greatness. The ideal of the hard-headed businessman went back to the same period when a succession of enterprising men seized the opportunities which opened before them with audacity and determination.

All these myths supported the city in its worst years, and helped to soften the consciousness of failure. Yet that was there, inescapably. Every Glaswegian has probably at some time sung Will Fyffe's 'I Belong tae Glasgow' with sentimental relish and with the sense of identification with the sentiments expressed. Fyffe's character is a loser, a Chaplinesque 'little man': he can take possession of his city only when he has 'had a couple of drinks on a Saturday'. He is the man put upon by circumstance, just as Glasgow is. A comparison between Will Fyffe and Billy Connolly shows a change in the temper of the city. Where Fyffe is resigned, Connolly is indignant. Fyffe makes defensive humour out of things as they are, and has no thought that they might be different. Connolly's humour is aggressive and challenging; he contrasts the way things are, with the way they should be. There is a new confidence and virility to his humour; he is a rebel, while Fyffe makes his humour out of defeat.

It is good to climb the Necropolis behind the Cathedral and gaze over the city of the living from this city of the dead. The hill is dominated by a huge statue of John Knox set, as it were, in opposition to the former Catholic Cathedral below; the statue was erected in the 1820s at the time of the movement for Catholic Emancipation, as an expression of Glasgow's stoutly Protestant faith; it was set up, therefore, shortly before immigration made Glasgow a city with one Catholic for every two Protestants. It makes a statement which has been subverted by history.

The Necropolis is, however, most distinctive as a repository of Victorian art and as a statement of Victorian confidence. The great family tombs of merchants and industrialists proclaim the wealth, and imitate the swagger, of the city. This is something rare in Britain: an aristocracy of commerce. The Necropolis is as impressive as Père Lachaise in Paris, but the best comparison is with the Campo Formo in Genoa, where angels mingle with gentlemen in top-hats and frock-coats. The revival of Glasgow is associated in the popular mind with the opening of the Burrell Collection, but to understand what made the Burrell Collection possible, to acquire a feel for the structure of the society which created and supported his wealth, the tourist should spend an afternoon on the Necropolis.

From its height you can see the whole city spread below: the sinuous ribbon of the Clyde, the dismantled shipyards, the few cranes still swinging their mighty loads into place, the tower-blocks, the parks, the Cathedral itself and the spires and towers of countless churches, the terraces which rise to the University on Gilmorehill, and beyond, the hills which enclose Glasgow on three sides and the Firth stretching out into the Atlantic, Glasgow's old empire. You are aware, on the Necropolis, that Glasgow is a great city on the fringe of the urban world; that it is a city which grew in response to circumstance and opportunity, and that it is one which has remained provisional, as cities with a political function never are. Such cities in the modern world are immune to contraction, for the ever-growing state acts as a preserving instrument. Glasgow, as the Necropolis reminds you with its litany of 'merchant in Glasgow', 'manufacturer in Glasgow', made itself, and accordingly has to find its own means of self-preservation.

Politically it has remained, except for a brief moment in the 1970s when the Scottish National Party held the balance of power on the Council, a Labour city. The Local Government reorganisation of 1974 deprived it of numerous functions, and incorporated it in the new Strathclyde Region. The principal function left to Glasgow District Council was housing; and since an excessive concentration on the provision of council housing had accelerated economic decline this might have been expected to have unfortunate consequences. Yet Glasgow benefited from the abolition of Local Government boundaries that no longer corresponded to any economic reality. Urban and suburban Strathclyde was an economic unit as the old City of Glasgow was not. The loss of independent status was a blow to civic pride but the advantages were real; it was the outlying parts of Strathclyde Region which had occasion to question these reforms, not Glasgow.

The long Labour hegemony has been, on balance, beneficial. The disadvantages of one-party rule are evident: a tendency to corruption, managerial complacency, the creation of a bureaucracy resistant to change and protective of established interests. Yet Glasgow has found that security of office encourages councillors to think of themselves as Glaswegians first and party members second. It has contributed to the growth of habits of co-operation; business interests recognise that the Labour administration is a natural part of Glasgow life and are the more ready to accept that they must work with it. At the same time the administration has learned that the recovery of prosperity depends on preferring collaboration to divisive rhetoric.

The politicians tend therefore to be practical men rather than ideologues. The nature of Labour's support in Glasgow has always forced them in this direction: a Socialist education policy has been rendered impossible because of the importance of the Catholic vote; the party has accordingly never questioned the anomaly of educational segregation on religious lines. Pragmatism has, however, been evident more recently: a report on the possibility of making schools within the Region self-managing had been commissioned before the Conservative Party proposed the same thing. The pragmatism did not extend to collaboration with the Conservative Government on the establishment of a self-governing Technology Academy in the old Allan Glen's School, though the advantages of the scheme were realised by some Labour councillors. Opposition was justified by the argument that such an academy would cream many of the best pupils from the city's comprehensives, with detrimental consequences for standards there.

Homogeneity is prized in Glasgow because it has been difficult to achieve. The religious divide is still deep, though it is veiled by a common code of manners and a commonly held social ethos which operates in all areas of life from which religion can be excluded. It was notable that when rapidly rising rates of unemployment returned to Glasgow in the late 1970s and early 1980s, there was no revival of the overtly discriminatory practices which had been common earlier. Except among the extremists of both sides, the passing of time and the intermarriage of Roman Catholics and Protestants has made the old ethno-religious quarrels obsolete. By the 1970s more than 40 per cent of Roman Catholics were marrying spouses who were at least nominally Protestant. Indeed intermarriage means that for many people religious allegiance has become a matter of choice rather than strict heredity. In 1989 the signing by Rangers of the former Celtic player Maurice Johnston sparked off denunciations from the extremists of both camps; but Johnston is himself the son of a Protestant father and a Catholic mother. His habit of crossing himself when he scored a goal had been seen by some Rangers supporters as an act of deliberate provocation in his Celtic days, but on signing for the Ibrox club, he revealed that his father had always supported Rangers. The Johnston affair appeared to some to confirm that Glasgow was still, as the BBC World Service had put it in 1981, 'a city notorious for bigotry', but the outbursts of invective with which the news of his transfer was greeted may more probably represent the last flicker of an old fire. Certainly Rangers could hardly have abandoned their old exclusive policy in more spectacular fashion. Though both clubs will continue to have a minority of supporters who see football as a substitute for irreligious bigotry, and though both will for a long time continue to draw the bulk of their support from their own side of the old religious divide, the divisions can never be so clear-cut again.

Glasgow has long since absorbed its Irish. It has also successfully assimilated later groups of immigrants: Italians, Jews, Lithuanians. 'Upward social mobility' has hastened the process. The integration of the large Italian community was made easier by the fact that they shared a common religion with a large part of the city's population, but were at the same time Catholic without fanaticism. Their respect for family and their capacity for hard work also eased their settlement. In turn the Italian community found the ethos of Glasgow sympathetic. A Neapolitan lawyer once told me he felt at home immediately in Glasgow, whereas he had felt himself a foreigner in London: 'I like a city where the children play in the streets.'

It cannot be claimed that the latest groups of immigrants, mostly from the Indian subcontinent, at least by origin, have yet been assimilated. Nevertheless it was noticeable that when race riots broke out in several English cities – London, Birmingham, Bristol and Liverpool especially, in 1981 – there were no similar incidents in Glasgow, though many of the underlying social problems could be found there too. What is striking, however, is the manner in which Glasgow's sense of its own identity has remained unimpaired by immigration, and the extent to which immigrant groups have found it both easy and comfortable to fit into life there. Though there is no doubt that the Muslim religion imposes a barrier against rapid integration, the absence of the sense of historical enmity which existed between Protestant and Catholic makes racial disturbances less likely; nor has Muslim immigration been on a scale comparable to the nineteenth-century Catholic immigration. It does not threaten to change the character of the city or to challenge the established order of things.

ENVOI

Sceptics still question the reality of Glasgow's recovery. In an article in the *Independent Magazine* in February 1989, Ian Jack, one of the best of contemporary Scottish journalists, himself a Glaswegian, conceded that 'civic chauvinism and great injections of public money have made the best of a bad job' but considered that 'the result is little more than a brightly embroidered shroud .... Today the river, which for 200 years gave Glasgow its purpose, lies dead and empty; an ornamental pond for the mortgageable classes whose semi-detached houses brighten up the landscaped banks in new English red brick (no bold modernism here that houses the unmortgageable).' The same thing has happened in London's Docklands. 'But,' added Jack, 'at least in London one kind of international trade has replaced another, today's money for yesterday's commerce. Glasgow has had to fall back on self-advertisement and history.'

There is enough truth in what he says to give pause. Certainly Glasgow has not solved all its problems. Perhaps no city ever can, for new problems emerge to replace old ones. But in Glasgow many of the old problems themselves remain. Whatever the reality of Glasgow's revival, it has barely touched the lives of a large part of the population. The peripheral housing estates are still places where very few people would choose to live; they represent the failure of municipal Socialism as clearly, and almost as dramatically, as the old city-centre slums represented the social failure of Victorian capitalism. In both cases, as I have tried to show, the reasons for the failure were natural, understandable and the consequences of certain habits of mind.

Jack drew attention to the failures of late municipal Socialism. 'The death of Glasgow, at least in the city's most important incarnation as an intimate city which made large machines, came suddenly in the 1960s and was confused at the time with the promise of new life. Glasgow councillors flew out to Los Angeles and thought they saw the future in its freeways. The same men hired Sir Basil Spence and pointed him at Gorbals.'

The outcome, in his view, was failure: the old was destroyed, or died, and the new was sterile. The idea of Glasgow was celebrated: 'The recent non-consuming past is continually evoked in books, paintings, plays and film.' The people, however, have been left out. They did not need to be flattered in this way. 'They knew who they were. What they required was not identity but a better way of life. Many have still to receive it.'

That consideration, which is valid, should act as a brake on the triumphal cart of Glasgow's year in 1990 as Cultural Capital of Europe. For all the city's recent achievements, for all its reviving wealth, its splendid universities, its opera, theatres, galleries and renovation, too many of its people still wait for a better way of life; too many despair of ever finding one; too many of its adolescents are unemployed, too many of them lack the skills which make any rewarding employment possible. Too many have therefore gained nothing from Glasgow's recovery. To this extent the scepticism may seem justified.

Yet the sceptics' argument is insubstantial. It could have been applied equally to the period of 'the city's most important incarnation as an intimate city which made large machines'; the workers at St Rollox or in Lord Overtoun's chemical factory scarcely shared in the prosperity they helped create; thousands of slum dwellers in casual employment were hardly beneficiaries of Glasgow's rapidly expanding economy. Yet the economy was expanding to the benefit of huge numbers of people. It is a melancholy, but inescapable, fact that in any such economy the disparities between those who benefit and those who fail to do so will actually become greater.

In this case the sceptics are also romantics who cannot accept that the city's economic base is changing, and who hark back with longing to the brave days of glory, when the Clyde was 'the ideal place to build iron ships' and one could 'sail down Auden's "glade of cranes" hearing the riveting evidence that Glasgow still held a place near the centre of the mechanical world'. Their nostalgia is natural, debilitating and distorting.

Moreover, placing the point of change back in the 1960s, Jack's time-scale is both too short and too long. On the one hand, it glides over half a century of decline; on the other hand, it prematurely condemns the city's response – 'they thought they saw the future in its freeways'.

The process of adaptation is inevitably slow and chequered. It is not helped by the assumption made by some that Glasgow must move, or is moving, into a 'post-industrial age'. Glasgow remains a city with many and increasingly varied industries: a glance at the Directory which has been published by the Chamber of Commerce, for example, reveals the extent of this variety. But it has developed in other directions too.

A modern city is a far more complex thing than a nineteenth-century one, just as the great Victorian manufacturing cities were far more complex, far less capable of being understood as a coherent whole, than the Glasgow which Defoe visited and summed up. Nor is understanding aided by a tendency to disparage certain kinds of economic activity as unsuitable, undesirable or unproductive – as being little more than 'toy jobs'. The location of Government departments in a city may appear dull, but even Government departments generate economic activity by their purchasing policy and by increasing the spending power of those whom they employ. Capital cities such as London, Paris, Rome and Washington have all benefited, at least in the sense of becoming richer, from the location of Government departments there. The policy of dispersing Government offices from London was adopted by the Labour Government of 1964–70 as part of its programme for 'regional' development. It is once again being practised, and more convincingly now, for the first dispersal was undertaken as a result of intellectually conceived policy, whereas the new round is coming about as a consequence of economic circumstance.

The revival of Glasgow will owe more to such circumstances than to intellectual concepts. Market forces made Glasgow great and rich in the nineteenth century; market forces brought about its comparative decline, market forces are now working in its favour. As the South-East of England, and London in particular, grows ever more congested, expensive and unsatisfactory, offering a deteriorating quality of life, economics and inclination come together to arrest the drift in that direction which has been a characteristic of this century. The reversal of that drift will aid Glasgow as it will the cities in the North of England.

It is being encouraged by political developments. The entry of Britain into the European Economic Community is having effects that go beyond the purely economic. It is leading to a new distribution of political power and influence. On the one hand the centripetal pull of the Community's institutions is reducing the importance of national capitals; on the other there are already signs that it will also lead to a devolution of authority to regional centres. This is likely to benefit Glasgow whether Scotland's position within the United Kingdom remains as it is, or not.

Advances in technology assist the process of dispersal by easing communications, reducing the importance of geographical concentration, and encouraging flexibility and diversification of business structures. Technological change has made size less important so that, for example, a provincial newspaper such as the *Glasgow Herald* can prosper on a circulation of around 120,000; thirty years ago it appeared that newspaper economics determined that the provincial press could only contract, and could survive only by curtailing its ambitions. Time and technology have exploded this notion. In the same way technological change is diluting the monopolistic tendencies of the big broadcasting organisations; the more numerous opportunities now available for independent producers, which this change has brought about, work to the advantage of provincial centres such as Glasgow.

The city that emerges from these changes, of which we are now only at the beginning, will be different from the one we have known. In point of size the difference will not be as significant as the changes which took place between 1707 and 1850. (Indeed it seems likely that the same processes of natural dispersal will cause the population within the boundaries of the old City of Glasgow to decline still further.) But in point of economic activity and social composition, they will be as important. The resemblance to other cities of the Northern Continent will be greater. Far more Glaswegians will work in offices, shops and other service industries, especially financial services, than will be employed making objects with their hands. This is already the case, but, as the memory of the great days of the Clyde recedes, and as the surviving shipbuilding industry is seen to take a small, though still significant and desirable, share of the city's economic activity, the change will come to seem natural and proper; though nostalgically minded romantics will still bewail, and even resent, what had happened, sensible people will approve.

The city will become less proletarian. The middle class will grow bigger, and middle-class values, which are still those of a consumer society, though increasingly concerned with environmental and conservationist issues, will become prevalent. It is easy to sneer at the transformation of the river into 'an ornamental pond for the mortgageable classes'; but a city requires mortgageable classes, and it has been Glasgow's misfortune in the twentieth century to possess an insufficiency of them. In short, it will become a city which would satisfy Dickson McCunn rather than revolutionary dreamers.

The success of this modern city will depend on the quality of education it can provide for its citizens. Glasgow starts with the advantage of two excellent universities. The University of Glasgow's Science Park will also ensure that the connection between the academic world and innovative industrial processes, which is an essential feature of economically-advanced societies, will be established and maintained. The University of Strathclyde runs a Business School. Other tertiary education is well-supplied. At school level, Glasgow had a long tradition of over-crowding. This is no longer the case. Indeed falling school rolls have compelled a policy of closures and amalgamations. This represents a loss of opportunity. More enlightened Government policy might have seen the fall in numbers as a chance to improve quality by improving teacher-pupil ratios. As it is, the policy of closures has inevitably created disaffection, while doing nothing to ameliorate the situation brought about by the creation of area comprehensives, which, inevitably as a result of housing policy, collect excessively large numbers of socially-disadvantaged children in particular schools; this can result in high levels of truancy and high numbers in individual schools who require remedial education. Despite the efforts of dedicated teachers, schools still tend to reflect the social polarisation established by housing policy. Yet it is their success – or failure – that will determine whether Glasgow can avoid the perpetuation of an underclass unable, because ill-equipped, to share in the city's returning prosperity.

The personality of Glasgow is such that it seems probable that changes in social structure and aspirations may be effected without changing the city's character. The strength of that character expresses itself in the pride that Glaswegians take in their city, and the love they feel for it. James Bridie, the dramatist and founder of the Citizens Theatre, whose name reflects that pride and love and whose achievements have done so much to justify them, once warned a correspondent not to patronise Glasgow: 'the city which gave the world the internal combustion engine, political economy, antiseptic, aseptic and cerebral surgery, the balloon, the mariner's compass, the Theory of Latent Heat, Tobias Smollett and James Bridie.' He could have added other names and other achievements.

The history of Glasgow is long and rich, but its year as Cultural Capital of Europe will be accounted a failure if it is not seen as marking the beginning of a new chapter as well as the summation of past achievements.

The three emblems associated with St Mungo, which appear on Glasgow's coat-of-arms, all represent rebirth. The lamps of the monastery had been extinguished; the saint took the frozen branch of a hazel and lit them again. The bird had been killed, torn in pieces by the saint's own followers, who should have guarded it; Mungo brought it back to life. The story of the salmon and the ring is a story about the loss of faith and trust: the king, suspecting his wife of infidelity, would have put her to death. The saint prevented this; by restoring the ring, he restored harmony and confidence.

It is not necessary to elaborate the metaphor, to draw detailed parallels between what these miracles represent and the history of Glasgow in the twentieth century. Suffice to say they have never seemed more timely in the fourteen hundred years since Mungo lived. The lamps had gone out, the city had torn itself to pieces, faith in its future was at a low ebb. But the miracle is taking place. The spirit of Mungo breathes on the city.

LET GLASGOW FLOURISH BY THE PREACHING OF THE WORD

AUTHOR'S NOTE

Rather than offer an extensive bibliography, I have restricted myself to books which I have found useful, and others which may be of interest for further reading.

Three authors require special mention. James Eagan's *History of Glasgow* (1862) is full of interesting and unusual information. The late Professor Sydney Checkland's short and brilliant study of industrial Glasgow, *The Upas Tree*, first aroused my interest in the subject, and I have drawn heavily on it. Like all who write on Scottish history I owe a debt to Professor T C Smout whose two volume *History of the Scottish People* (Collins 1969 & 1986) is a rich mine.

I also owe much to Michael Fry's political history of modern Scotland: *Patronage and Principle* (AUP 1987) and to the *Dictionary of Scottish Business Biography* (AUP 1986).

All writers on Glasgow owe a debt also to C M Oakley and Jack House; mine is considerable.

Chapter seven draw extensively on the autobiographies of John Buchan and Edwin Muir and on Sir Duncan Wilson's biography of Gilbert Murray (OUP 1987). Two of Buchan's novels, *Huntingtower* and *Mr Standfast* have also contributed to this chapter. So has Edwin Muir's *Scottish Journey*, and R F Mackenzie's *A Search for Scotland* (Collins 1989).

The novels of Guy McCrone, Neil Munro, George Blake, Alasdair Gray, James Kelman and William McIlvanney are all invaluable to an understanding of the city at different periods; as is of course Scott's *Rob Roy*. My chief debt to authors of fiction is owed however to Alan Spence and the authors of *No Mean City*, McAllister & Kingsley Long.

Chapter Nine, 'A City of Celts', could not have been written without John M Bannerman's posthumous *Memoirs*, edited by John Fowler.

I am grateful to Robert Clow for lending me a scrapbook which assisted my understanding of post-war developments in Glasgow, to Euan Cameron for his constant encouragement, to Duncan McAra for his scrupulous and intelligent editing of the text, and to Allan MacInnes of the Department of Scottish History at the University of Glasgow for suggesting emendations and corrections. Finally, my chief debt is as ever to my wife, Alison.

INDEX